A Character Profile Book
Group Book Report Project

1. Cut out the label and tabs. Glue them to six index cards.
2. Draw and write to complete each card.
3. Stack the cards. Punch holes and bind the pages with yarn.

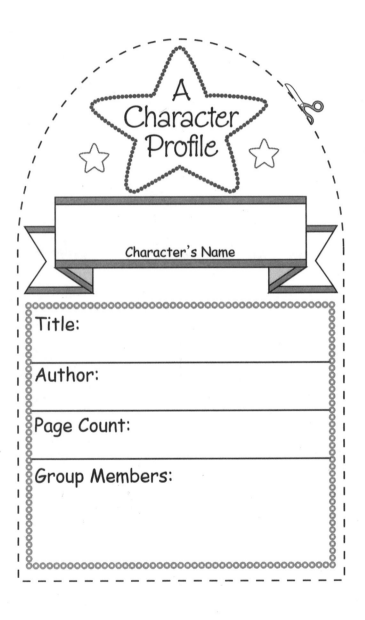

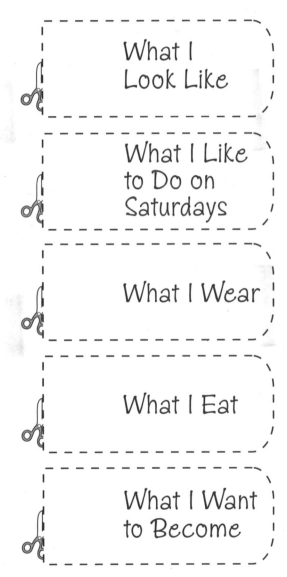

What I Look Like

What I Like to Do on Saturdays

What I Wear

What I Eat

What I Want to Become

Trivia Game

Group Book Report Project

Literature Skill Focus: Recalling story details

1. Giving the Assignment

- Ask students if they have ever played a trivia game. Discuss their experiences and the purpose of the game, which is to recall facts about an event or person. Tell students that they will be writing trivia questions about books.

- Model the process of turning a trivia fact into a question. Fact: The Monroe family found Bunnicula at the movie theater when they went to see the movie *Dracula*. Question: What movie were the Monroes going to see when Toby found Bunnicula?

2. Reading with a Small Group

- Assign students to work in small groups. Select several different books, and assign one book to each group. Provide a copy for each member. Each student reads the book independently.

- In their groups, students discuss the book. They create a master list of trivia questions and answers. Group members copy the questions and answers onto index cards for the trivia game.

3. Sharing the Group Projects

- Display the trivia questions with a copy of each book.

- As students read each book, have them play the trivia game.

How to Make Trivia Cards

1. Think of a trivia fact. Write the fact as a question on the master list on page 75. Write the answer on the list. Repeat for at least fifteen questions.

2. Copy the trivia questions onto 3" x 5" (7.5 x 13 cm) index cards. At the bottom of the cards, write the name of the book and the page where the answer can be found. Write the answer on the back. (To facilitate sorting, each group could use index cards of different colors.)

3. Check the information on the cards and the master trivia list to make sure that they match.

Question: What movie were the Monroes going to see when Toby found Bunnicula?

Answer: Dracula

Book Report Forms

Fiction or Nonfiction?
Book Report Form
Literature Skill Focus: Determining whether a story is fiction or nonfiction

1. Teaching the Literature Skill

- Collect several books on the same topic. Pick some books that are fiction and some that are nonfiction. Ask students to tell you what they know about the difference between fiction and nonfiction. List the characteristics students suggest on a chart or the chalkboard.

- Read a book to your class that is obviously fiction. For example, *Dragonfly's Tale* by Kristina Rodanas is a folk tale based on a Zuni legend. It emphasizes respect for nature. After being wasteful, the Ashiwi tribe suffers a poor harvest. Two children are left behind as the tribe searches for food. The boy makes a cornhusk dragonfly to entertain his sister, and he regains the Corn Maiden's blessings. Ask students if this story is real or imaginary. Have them give specific examples from the book that support their opinions. Lead them to see that this book is fiction.

- Read *Dragonflies* by Cheryl Coughlan to your class. The photographs and text introduce the physical features of dragonflies. Ask students if this book is real or imaginary. Lead them to the conclusion that the photographs and content of the book indicate that it is factual, or true. It is nonfiction.

- Next, analyze several realistic fiction books. *Eliza and the Dragonfly* by Susie Caldwell Rinehart is a good example. It is a story of a girl who observes the life cycle of the dragonfly. The author presents factual information in the context of a fiction story. Help your students to see that factual information can be found in fiction books.

2. Reading Independently

- Have students choose a book from the library. They take the book home to read independently. The student completes the form on page 3 and returns it to school.

3. Sharing the Book Reports

- When the book reports have been returned, display them, have a class discussion about the literature skill in students' books, or have partners share their books.

Good Books to Read

Cheyenne Indians
The Cheyennes by Virginia Driving Hawk Sneve
Death of the Iron Horse by Paul Goble
Her Seven Brothers by Paul Goble

Dragonflies
Dragonflies by Cheryl Coughlan
Dragonfly's Tale by Kristina Rodanas
Eliza and the Dragonfly by Susie Caldwell Rinehart

Flies
A Book of Flies Real or Otherwise by Richard Michelson
Old Black Fly by Jim Aylesworth

Libraries
Richard Wright and the Library Card by William Miller
Goin' Someplace Special by Patricia C. McKissack

Math
Division by Sheila Cato
A Remainder of One by Elinor J. Pinczes

Note: Nonfiction selections listed first.

Name_____

Fiction or Nonfiction?
Book Report Form

Title:

Author:	Illustrator:

Were there any facts in the story?   yes   no

If your answer is yes, give an example.

Was the story fiction or nonfiction?   ☐ fiction   ☐ nonfiction

Tell why you think the story is fiction or nonfiction.

And the Star Is...
Book Report Form

Literature Skill Focus: Identifying and describing the main character in a story

1. Teaching the Literature Skill

- Briefly review the term *character* with your students. Explain that a book usually has one or two important, or main, characters.

- Read chapters 1 and 2 of *Dear Napoleon, I Know You're Dead, But...* by Elvira Woodruff to your class. The book is a story about the relationship between a fourth-grader and his grandfather. Ask students to name the characters from the excerpt. They are Marty, Miss Gerbino, Russell, Jessica, and Grandpa. List these on a chart or the chalkboard. Then have students identify the person they think is the main character. The students should be ready to support their choices with examples from the story. For example, the story focuses on Marty's letters, his grandfather, and his friends, so Marty must be the main character.

- Model how to write a short description of Marty. For example, Martin Bellucci is a fourth-grade student at Midbury Elementary School in New Hampshire. Marty loves history and isn't afraid to be a little different than everyone else. He also wants to be in the *Guinness Book of World Records*.

- Ask students if they think their description of the main character might change if they read the entire book. Complete the book as a read-aloud and answer the question as a class.

2. Reading Independently

- Have students choose a fiction book from the library. They take the book home to read independently. The students complete the form on page 5 and return it to school.

3. Sharing the Book Reports

- When the book reports have been returned, display them, have a class discussion about the literature skill in the students' books, or have partners share their books.

Good Books to Read

The Boyhood Diary of Charles A. Lindbergh, 1913–1916: Early Adventures of the Famous Aviator by Charles Lindbergh

Call Me Ahnighito by Pam Conrad

Chester the Worldly Pig by Bill Peet

Dear Napoleon, I Know You're Dead, But... by Elvira Woodruff

Horrible Harry and the Mud Gremlins by Suzy Kline

Lucy Rose, Here's the Thing About Me by Katy Kelly

Max's Logbook by Marissa Moss

Mean Margaret by Tor Seidler

Name_____

And the Star Is...
Book Report Form

Title:

Author:

Who is the main character in the book?

Write several sentences to describe the character.

Tell why you think this character is the most important.

Friends to the End
Book Report Form

Literature Skill Focus: Recognizing relationships between characters

1. Teaching the Literature Skill

- Briefly review the term *character* with your students. Explain that a story usually reveals the relationships between the characters. Have students brainstorm possible relationships, such as friends, acquaintances, schoolmates, neighbors, and family members. Record their ideas.

- Read the first chapter of *Zippity Zinger* by Henry Winkler and Lin Oliver. The story tells about fourth-grader Hank Zipzer and his dilemma with some "lucky" socks.

- Have students identify the characters in the story and discuss the relationships between the characters. The characters are Hank, his sister, his grandfather, and his friends. Model how to write a few sentences about the relationship between two characters who are friends in the story. For example, Hank's best friend, Frankie, believes that Hank can pitch for the class team. Even when Hank is not sure of his own ability, Frankie supports him.

2. Reading Independently

- Have students choose a fiction book from the library. They take the book home to read independently. The students complete the form on page 7 and return it to school.

3. Sharing the Book Reports

- When the book reports have been returned, display them, have a class discussion about the literature skill in the students' books, or have partners share their books.

Good Books to Read

The Bicycle Man by Allen Say

The Good Dog by Avi

The Old Woman Who Named Things by Cynthia Rylant

Seven Brave Women by Betsy Hearne

The Sweetest Fig by Chris Van Allsburg

A Toad for Tuesday by Russell E. Erickson

Zippity Zinger by Henry Winkler and Lin Oliver

Name_____

Friends to the End
Book Report Form

Title:

Author:

Illustrator:

List the characters in the story.
Put stars by the main characters.

Write about two characters who are friends.
Draw them in the frame.

Which character would you like to
have as a friend? Tell why.

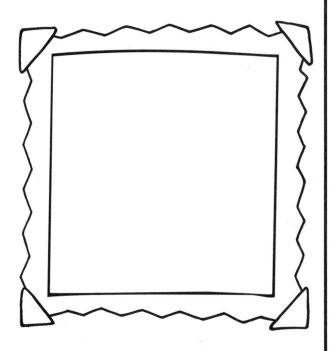

Guess Who!

Book Report Form

Literature Skill Focus: Describing a character

1. Teaching the Literature Skill

- Briefly review the idea that there is often one character in a story that is most important. Explain that this character is called the main character. Discuss with students the different kinds of things they learn about story characters, such as what they like to do, how they feel, what they look like, and why they do what they do. List the categories students suggest on a chart or the chalkboard.

- Then read *Miss Rumphius* by Barbara Cooney. The story traces the life of a woman from girlhood to old age. It tells how she makes the world a more beautiful place.

- Using the categories that you discussed earlier, have students recall what they learned about Alice Rumphius. Using students' ideas, model how to write a riddle with three clues. Include at least one clue about what Miss Rumphius looked like and one clue about something she did.

2. Reading Independently

- Have students choose a fiction book from the library. They take the book home to read independently. The students complete the form on page 9 and return it to school.

3. Sharing the Book Reports

- When the book reports have been returned, display them, have a class discussion about the literature skill in the students' books, or have partners share their books.

Good Books to Read

The A+ Custodian by Louise Borden

Bottle Houses: The Creative World of Grandma Prisbrey by Melissa Eskridge Slaymaker

Harry Kitten and Tucker Mouse by George Selden

Hobart by Anita Briggs

Miss Lady Bird's Wildflowers: How a First Lady Changed America by Kathi Appelt

Miss Rumphius by Barbara Cooney

The Mouse of Amherst by Elizabeth Spires

Snowflake Bentley by Jacqueline Briggs Martin

Name_____

Guess Who!
Book Report Form

Title: _____

Author: _____

Illustrator: _____

Write a riddle about one character in your book.

_____

_____

_____

_____

Give three clues.
Write one clue about what the character looked like and one clue about something the character did.

1. _____

_____

2. _____

_____

3. _____

_____

Destination: Good Reading

Book Report Form

Literature Skill Focus: Identifying location as part of the story setting

1. Teaching the Literature Skill

- Review the term *setting* with your students. Remind them that the setting of a story is the time and place a story occurs. Ask students to focus on the location of the story you read to them.

- Read *Moses the Kitten* by James Herriot. The story is about a young kitten that Mr. Herriot rescues. It is adopted by a Yorkshire farmer and his wife. Have students listen for clues to the location as you read. For example, snowy, windy, farm gate, uncharitable world, frozen pond off the path, and rime-covered rushes. Some students might mention Mr. Butler's way of talking.

- Ask students to think about where the story is taking place. Is it in an urban or rural setting? Is it in the U.S. or another country? Have them support their ideas with clues from the story. Students should be able to deduce that the story takes place in an unpopulated, rural setting in England. The book jacket will confirm that the story is set on a wintry day in Yorkshire, England.

- Discuss how location affects a story. Ask students what they would do if they found themselves in this location.

2. Reading Independently

- Have students choose a fiction book from the library. They take the book home to read independently. The students complete the form on page 11 and return it to school.

3. Sharing the Book Reports

- When the book reports have been returned, display them, have a class discussion about the literature skill in the students' books, or have partners share their books.

Good Books to Read

The Drinking Gourd: A Story of the Underground Railroad by F. N. Monjo

Freddy and the Space Ship by Walter R. Brooks

Ghosts of the White House by Cheryl Harness

Mojave by Diane Siebert

Moses the Kitten by James Herriot

Seaman: The Dog Who Explored the West with Lewis & Clark by Gail Langer Karwoski

Silver Packages: An Appalachian Christmas Story by Cynthia Rylant

What You Know First by Patricia MacLachlan

Good Book Ahead!

Name_____

Destination: Good Reading
Book Report Form

Title:	
Author:	Illustrator:

Describe the location of the story.

If you went to this location, what would you do?

When and Where?
Book Report Form

Literature Skill Focus: Identifying the setting and comparing it to the setting of students' lives

1. Teaching the Literature Skill

- Review the term *setting* with your students. The setting is the time and place a story occurs. Discuss how setting contributes to a story. For example, the setting adds details to a story. A story might turn out differently depending on where and when it happens.

- Read the first chapter of *Bud, Not Buddy* by Christopher Paul Curtis. Have students describe the setting at the beginning of the story. Students might say that the story takes place in an orphanage or foster home during hard times.

- Ask students to identify the setting of their own lives. Ask them to compare that setting with the one in *Bud, Not Buddy*. How are the two alike? How are the two different? Could Buddy's story have happened in the time and place in which your students live? How would the story have changed?

2. Reading Independently

- Have students choose a fiction book from the library. They take the book home to read independently. The students complete the form on page 13 and return it to school.

3. Sharing the Book Reports

- When the book reports have been returned, display them, have a class discussion about the literature skill in the students' books, or have partners share their books.

Good Books to Read

Bud, Not Buddy by Christopher Paul Curtis

The Day Gogo Went to Vote by Elinor Batezat Sisulu

Diary of a Little Girl in Old New York by Catherine Elizabeth Havens

Don't You Know There's a War On? by Avi

Hooray for Diffendoofer Day! by Dr. Seuss

Out of the Dust by Karen Hesse

Smoky Night by Eve Bunting

What is the setting?

When and Where?
Book Report Form

Title:	
Author:	Illustrator:
When did the story happen?	Where did the story happen?

Compare the setting of the book to your neighborhood today.

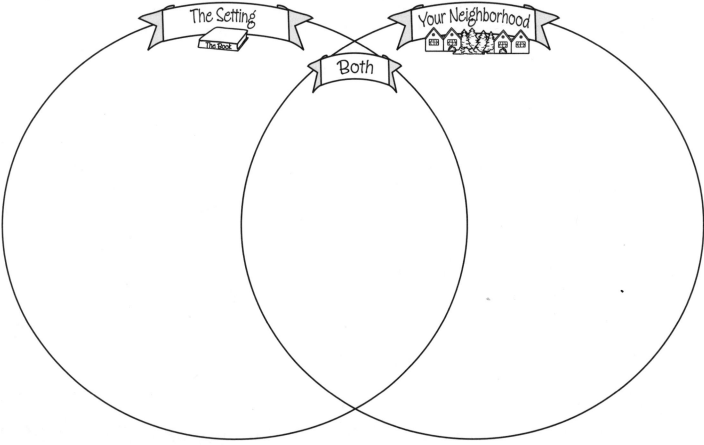

Map the Action
Book Report Form

Literature Skill Focus: Mapping the story's plot

1. Teaching the Literature Skill

- Introduce the term *plot* to your students. The plot is the action of the story. The action is a series of events called the plotline. The plotline usually includes a beginning, a middle, a climax, and an ending. The beginning is where the setting, the characters, and the problem or conflict are introduced. In the middle, the main character tries to solve his or her problem. The climax, or turning point, is the most exciting or important part of the story. The ending, or resolution, is when the problem is solved.

- Read the folk tale *Sukey and the Mermaid* by Robert D. San Souci. Map the plot on a transparency copy of page 15.

  Beginning: Sukey lives with her mother and stepfather on a little island off the coast of South Carolina. Sukey is very unhappy because her stepfather makes her work all the time. Sukey discovers a mermaid who gives her a gold coin for her parents. Sukey promises to keep the mermaid a secret.

  Middle: Sukey's mother and stepfather try to catch the mermaid to get more gold coins. Sukey has to work until she is sick. The mermaid takes Sukey to her home under the sea. Sukey misses other humans. The mermaid returns Sukey to land with a bag of gold and tells Sukey to marry a man named Dembo.

  Climax: Stepfather kills Dembo to get the treasure.

  End: Mermaid gives Sukey a seed pearl to bring Dembo back to life. Stepfather flees and is swallowed by the sea. Sukey and Dembo find the treasure and live happily ever after.

2. Reading Independently

- Have students choose a fiction book from the library. They take the book home to read independently. The students complete the form on page 15 and return it to school.

3. Sharing the Book Reports

- When the book reports have been returned, display them, have a class discussion about the literature skill in the students' books, or have partners share their books.

Good Books to Read

The Amazing Christmas Extravaganza by David Shannon

Black and White by David Macaulay

The Capture by Kathryn Lasky

Comet's Nine Lives by Jan Brett

Fortunately by Remy Charlip

Leonardo's Horse by Jean Fritz

Sukey and the Mermaid by Robert D. San Souci

The Volcano Disaster by Peg Kehret

Wow! What a plot!

How to Report on Books • EMC 6009 • © Evan-Moor Corp.

Map the Action
Book Report Form

Title:

Author:	Illustrator:

The Beginning—characters, setting, problem

The Middle—how did the character try to solve the problem?

The Climax—the most exciting part

The End—how was the problem solved?

Write a summary of the story's action.

The Problem Is Solved

Book Report Form

Literature Skill Focus: Identifying the story's problem and solution

1. Teaching the Literature Skill

- Read chapter 1 of *Charlotte's Web* by E. B. White. Ask students to identify the problem and solution presented in the chapter. For example, the problem is that Fern wants to save the runt of the pig litter from her father's ax. The solution is that Fern's father gives the runt to Fern to raise.

- Discuss how the author introduced the problem, what Fern did, and the solution. For example, E. B. White introduces the problem in the first sentence when Fern asks, "Where's Papa going with that ax?" Fern tries to wrestle the ax away from her father. Fern feels that killing a pig just because he's small is unfair. Her father understands his daughter's compassion for the runt, so he gives the pig to Fern to raise. Fern falls in love with her pig.

- Explain that sometimes there is more than one problem in a chapter book. Have students write their book report about the main problem in the story.

2. Reading Independently

- Have students choose a fiction book from the library. They take the book home to read independently. The students complete the form on page 17 and return it to school.

3. Sharing the Book Reports

- When the book reports have been returned, display them, have a class discussion about the literature skill in the students' books, or have partners share their books.

Good Books to Read

Among the Hidden by Margaret Peterson Haddix

Babe: The Gallant Pig by Dick King-Smith

Brave Irene by William Steig

Brave Margaret: An Irish Adventure by Robert D. San Souci

Charlotte's Web by E. B. White

Farewell to Shady Glade by Bill Peet

Letting Swift River Go by Jane Yolen

Rikki-Tikki-Tavi by Rudyard Kipling and illustrated by Jerry Pinkney

Name_____

The Problem Is Solved
Book Report Form

Title:

Author: Illustrator:

⭐ Main Character:

The Problem:

How the character tried to solve the problem:

① ② ③

The Solution

...Happily Ever After

Book Report Form

Literature Skill Focus: Evaluating if a story ending is a happy one

1. Teaching the Literature Skill

- Read *The Full Belly Bowl* by Jim Aylesworth to your class. Ask students to retell the ending. For example, the cats break the Full Belly Bowl. The old man promised himself that he would be more careful, and he continued to live in a tiny house with the sweetest cats in the world.

- Ask students to decide whether they think the ending was happy or not. They should support their opinion with examples from the story. Students may say that the story ending was happy because the old man loved his cats and was satisfied living in the little house at the edge of the woods. Or, students may say that the ending was unhappy because the Full Belly Bowl was broken and the old man was as poor as ever. If students do not point out the two opposing viewpoints, support one of the viewpoints yourself to encourage discussion.

2. Reading Independently

- Have students choose a fiction book from the library. They take the book home to read independently. The students complete the form on page 19 and return it to school.

3. Sharing the Book Reports

- When the book reports have been returned, display them, have a class discussion about the literature skill in students' books, or have partners share their books.

Good Books to Read

Baseball Saved Us by Ken Mochizuki

Everyone Knows What a Dragon Looks Like by Jay Williams

The Full Belly Bowl by Jim Aylesworth

Ghosts of the Civil War by Cheryl Harness

Jackalope by Janet Stevens and Susan Stevens Crummel

Piggie Pie! by Margie Palatini

Stone Fox by John Reynolds Gardiner

Sun & Spoon by Kevin Henkes

...Happily Ever After
Book Report Form

Title:

Author:	Illustrator:

Retell the ending of the book.

Do you think this is a happy ending?   yes   no

Support your opinion with an example from the story.

A New Ending
Book Report Form
Literature Skill Focus: Creating an alternate ending to a story

1. Teaching the Literature Skill

- Read *Little Oh* by Laura Krauss Melmed to your class. This "Pinocchio tale" tells the story of a lonely woman who folds paper into an origami child. The origami child changes into a real daughter.

- Have your students retell the ending of the story. Then ask them to think of another way the story might end. For example, as he bowed, the man held out the paper heart. Just as the woman reached for it, a gust of wind stole the heart and tossed it into the air. Magically, the heart became a lovely bird that chirped as it dipped its wings and flew away. The woman gasped and nodded to the man and the boy.

- Take the time to share several new endings.

2. Reading Independently

- Have students choose a fiction book from the library. They take the book home to read independently. The students complete the form on page 21 and return it to school.

3. Sharing the Book Reports

- When the book reports have been returned, display them, have a class discussion about the literature skill in students' books, or have partners share their books.

Good Books to Read

Anansi and the Magic Stick by Eric A. Kimmel

Baloney (Henry P.) by Jon Scieszka

Harry on the Rocks by Susan Meddaugh

Horton Hatches the Egg by Dr. Seuss

Joey Pigza Swallowed the Key by Jack Gantos

Little Oh by Laura Krauss Melmed

Star in the Storm by Joan Hiatt Harlow

Tell Me a Scary Story… But Not TOO Scary! by Carl Reiner

Try a new ending!

Name_____

A New Ending
Book Report Form

Title:

Author: | Illustrator:

Retell the ending of the story as it is in the book.

Write another ending for the story.

The Bare Facts

Book Report Form

Literature Skill Focus: Identifying story elements

1. Teaching the Literature Skill

- Review the story elements you will be asking students to identify. These are the title, author, illustrator, setting, main characters, problem, and solution.

- Read *Emily* by Michael Bedard. Help students identify the elements in the story.

  Setting: 1800s; *Amherst, Massachusetts*

  Characters: the Myth (Emily Dickinson); young girl; girl's mother and father

  Problem: woman lives across the street who refuses all visitors

  Solution: the young girl makes friends with her

- Ask students if they liked the story and have them support their opinions with reasons. Model how to write the reasons. For example, I liked *Emily* because the story was mysterious. You didn't know what kind of person the Myth was going to be, or what the Myth looked like.

2. Reading Independently

- Have students choose a fiction book from the library. They take the book home to read independently. The students complete the form on page 23 and return it to school.

3. Sharing the Book Reports

- When the book reports have been returned, display them, have a class discussion about the literature skill in students' books, or have partners share their books.

Good Books to Read

Any Small Goodness: A Novel of the Barrio by Tony Johnston

The Arrow Over the Door by Joseph Bruchac

The Courage of Sarah Noble by Alice Dalgliesh

Emily by Michael Bedard

Hannah's Journal: The Story of an Immigrant Girl by Marissa Moss

High as a Hawk: A Brave Girl's Historic Climb by T. A. Barron

Merlin and the Dragons by Jane Yolen

Swamp Angel by Anne Isaacs

What are the facts?

The Bare Facts
Book Report Form

Title:

Author: Illustrator:

Setting:

Characters: Problem:

Solution:.   Did you like the story?   yes   no
                                 Give 2 reasons why or why not.

                                 1.

                                 2.

Rating a Book
Book Report Form

Literature Skill Focus: Evaluating literature by rating character, plot, and ending

1. Teaching the Literature Skill

- Explain to students that this book report focuses on their opinions. They will be rating the story elements by using bar graphs. The quality of the book report will depend on the reasons given for the ratings.

- Read *Fly Away Home* by Eve Bunting. This story takes place in a busy airport in contemporary times. The main characters are Andrew and his dad. Other characters are the members of the Medina family—Danny, Grandma, and Mrs. Medina. The little brown bird is also an important character. The plot revolves around the characters' daily life in the airport, how they wash up, where they eat and sleep, and how they go unnoticed. At the end, the bird flies free.

- Identify the story elements on the top of a sample form. Then fill in the bar graphs to rate the book. Write a supporting sentence for each rating.

2. Reading Independently

- Have students choose a fiction book from the library. They take the book home to read independently. The students complete the form on page 25 and return it to school.

3. Sharing the Book Reports

- When the book reports have been returned, display them, have a class discussion about the literature skill in students' books, or have partners share their books.

Good Books to Read

Atlantis: The Legend of a Lost City by Christina Balit

Birdbrain Amos by Michael Delaney

Bunnicula Strikes Again! by James Howe

Fly Away Home by Eve Bunting

Frindle by Andrew Clements

The Ghost in Room 11 by Betty Ren Wright

Miss Alaineus: A Vocabulary Disaster by Debra Frasier

Somewhere in the World Right Now by Stacey Schuett

How would I rate this?

How to Report on Books • EMC 6009 • © Evan-Moor Corp.

Name_____

Rating a Book
Book Report Form

Title:	
Author:	Illustrator:
Setting:	

Color the bar graphs to rate this book.

Characters 1 is **not recommended**   5 is **okay**   10 is **good**

Were they interesting? Did you feel that you knew them?

_____

_____

Plot

Was it exciting? Did you want to know what was going to happen next?

_____

_____

Ending

Was it the best ending for the story?

_____

_____

Recommend It to a Friend

Book Report Form

Literature Skill Focus: Writing a recommendation

1. Teaching the Literature Skill

- Ask students how they choose books that they want to read. They might say favorite author, interesting topic, picture on the cover, or someone's recommendation. Explain that they will be writing a recommendation for a book they read.

- As a class, brainstorm the features of a good recommendation. For example, it tells a little, but not too much, about the book. A good recommendation gives the correct author and title so it is easy to find the book. It gives specific details about the book, such as "The descriptions in the story were so good that I had a picture of Grandma in my head. I understood Julia and Daniel's excitement when they found the dinosaur bones."

- Read a portion of *My Daniel* by Pam Conrad to the class. Using the brainstormed ideas, model how to write a recommendation.

2. Reading Independently

- Have students choose a book from the library. They take the book home to read independently. The students complete the form on page 27 and return it to school.

3. Sharing the Book Reports

- When the book reports have been returned, display them, have a class discussion about the literature skill in students' books, or have partners share their books.

Good Books to Read

Anno's Journey by Mitsumasa Anno

G is for Googol: A Math Alphabet Book by David M. Schwartz

I'm in Charge of Celebrations by Byrd Baylor

My Daniel by Pam Conrad

The Spirit of the Maasai Man by Laura Berkeley

Squids Will Be Squids: Fresh Morals, Beastly Fables by Jon Scieszka

When Pigasso Met Mootisse by Nina Laden

The Witches by Roald Dahl

I understood Julia and Daniel's excitement when they found the dinosaur bones!

Name _____

Recommend It to a Friend
Book Report Form

This is a good book!

Title:

Author:

Illustrator: Page count:

I liked the book for these reasons:

I'm going to tell my friend _____ about this one!
(name)

My Book Diary

Book Report Form

Literature Skill Focus: Tracking reading progress and identifying story elements

1. Teaching the Literature Skill

- Explain to students that they will be keeping a log, or diary, about the book they are reading. A diary is a daily record. Each time the student reads, he or she will record the date and the pages read. The student will make notes about the story elements.

- Choose a book and model how to record the title, illustrator, and author on the book report form. Write the date and beginning page number. Read several pages, make notes about the story elements, and record the ending page number.

2. Reading Independently

- Have students choose a fiction book from the library. They take the book home to read independently. The students complete the form on page 29 and return it to school.

3. Sharing the Book Reports

- When the book reports have been returned, display them, have a class discussion about the literature skill in students' books, or have partners share their books.

Good Books to Read

Bartleby of the Mighty Mississippi by Phyllis Shalant

The Diary of Melanie Martin: Or How I Survived Matt the Brat, Michelangelo, and the Leaning Tower of Pizza by Carol Weston

The Fortune-Tellers by Lloyd Alexander

Henry and the Kite Dragon by Bruce Edward Hall

Judy Moody Declares Independence by Megan McDonald

One Lucky Summer by Laura McGee Kvasnosky

The Worst Band in the Universe by Graeme Base

Today I began a new book!

Name_____

My Book Diary
Book Report Form

Today I began a new book!

Title:

Author: Illustrator:

Each time I read I discover something new.

My Reading Log		
Date	**Pages Read**	**Notes on the Book**
		Characters:
		Setting:
		Plot:

I rate this book: good   fair   poor

My Favorite Author

Book Report Form

Literature Skill Focus: Learning about an author

1. Teaching the Literature Skill

- Choose several books from your library by a favorite author. Share the books with your students. Tell a little about the author and why you like to read the author's books. Show your students where to locate information about the author on the book jacket.

- For example, if you picked Ed Young, he wrote *Lon Po Po, Mouse Match,* and *Seven Blind Mice.* Ed Young was born in China in 1931. Mr. Young loved reading and drawing. He made up plays, as well. Ed Young's real name is Tse-chun. He says that his daughter helped him think about books from a child's point of view. I like Ed Young's stories because they have a moral and his pictures complement his beautiful words.

2. Reading Independently

- Have students choose a book from the library. They take the book home to read independently. The students complete the form on page 31 and return it to school.

3. Sharing the Book Reports

- When the book reports have been returned, display them, have a class discussion about the literature skill in students' books, or have partners share their books.

Good Books to Read

Betsy Byars
The Midnight Fox
The Moon & I
The SOS File

Jerry Pallotta
Dory Story
The Ocean Alphabet Book
Read a Zillion Books

Dav Pilkey
The Adventures of Captain Underpants
Dogzilla
World War Won

Cynthia Rylant
Best Wishes
Christmas in the Country
Waiting to Waltz: A Childhood

Ed Young
Lon Po Po
Mouse Match
Seven Blind Mice

William Steig
CDB!
Shrek!
When Everybody Wore a Hat

How to Report on Books • EMC 6009 • © Evan-Moor Corp.

Name_____

My Favorite Author
Book Report Form

Author's Name:

┌─────────────────────────────────┐
│ **About the Author** │
│ │
│ │
│ │
│ │
│ │
│ │
│ │
└─────────────────────────────────┘

┌─────────────────────────────────┐
│ **Books by the Author** │
│ │
│ │
│ │
│ │
│ │
│ │
│ │
└─────────────────────────────────┘

┌───┐
│ **Why I like to read this author's books** │
│ │
│ │
│ │
│ │
└───┘

Prizewinning Illustrators

Book Report Form

Literature Skill Focus: Recognizing the importance of illustrations in a story

1. Teaching the Literature Skill

- Lead a discussion about the importance of illustrations in telling a story. If your students are not familiar with the Caldecott Medal, explain that each year, the medal is given to an illustrator of children's picture books.

- Show your students several books that have the Caldecott Medal on the cover.

- Explain that the focus of this book report is on the illustrator and the illustrations, as well as the story.

- Read *Owl Moon* by Jane Yolen. Show students John Schoenherr's beautiful illustrations. Point out that Mr. Schoenherr likes to use strong colors and shapes to develop a picture, rather than a lot of details. Have students explain how the illustrations enhance the story. Model how to write this in a sentence. For example, the blue hills and lighter blue snow make the story feel cold.

2. Reading Independently

- Have students choose a Caldecott Award-winning book from the library. They take the book home to read independently. The students complete the form on page 33 and return it to school.

3. Sharing the Book Reports

- When the book reports have been returned, display them, have a class discussion about the literature skill in students' books, or have partners share their books.

Good Books to Read

Books by Illustrators:

Lynne Cherry
Making a Difference in the World
The Sea, the Storm, and the Mangrove Tangle
The Shaman's Apprentice: A Tale of the Amazon Rain Forest

Peter H. Reynolds
The Dot
Ish
The North Star

Faith Ringgold
Cassie's Word Quilt
Tar Beach

Chris Van Allsburg
Bad Day at Riverbend
The Mysteries of Harris Burdick

David Wiesner
The Loathsome Dragon
Tuesday

Books About Illustrators:

Pat Cummings
Talking with Artists

Leonard S. Marcus
A Caldecott Celebration: Six Artists and Their Paths to the Caldecott Medal

Jennifer Tarr Coyne
Discovering Women Artists for Children

How to Report on Books • EMC 6009 • © Evan-Moor Corp.

Prizewinning Illustrators
Book Report Form

Caldecott
_____
Year
Winner

Title:
Author:
Illustrator:

The illustrations are:

____ drawings   ____ stitched

____ paintings   ____ black and white

____ collages   ____ color

I learned 3 facts about the illustrator.

1. _____

_____

2. _____

_____

3. _____

_____

Tell why you think the illustrations are important to the story.

Parent Letter
Support Independent Reading

Dear Parent,

Even though your child has been reading independently for some time, you are still important to supporting his or her love of reading. There are several ways you can do this. Ask your child to tell you about the books he or she has checked out of the school library. Ask how well he or she is enjoying the books. Your child will be asked to do a report, an individual project, or a group project on a book. Share a book with your child by reading aloud to each other. Discuss the characters and the plot. Savor this time together. You are the most influential person in your child's life.

Sincerely,

Dear Parent,

Even though your child has been reading independently for some time, you are still important to supporting his or her love of reading. There are several ways you can do this. Ask your child to tell you about the books he or she has checked out of the school library. Ask how well he or she is enjoying the books. Your child will be asked to do a report, an individual project, or a group project on a book. Share a book with your child by reading aloud to each other. Discuss the characters and the plot. Savor this time together. You are the most influential person in your child's life.

Sincerely,

Individual Book Report Projects

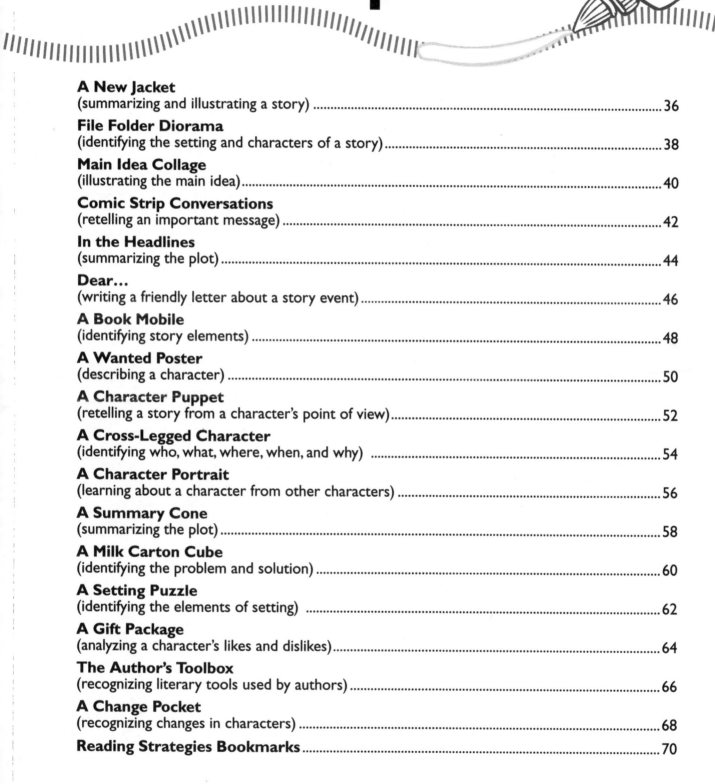

A New Jacket

Individual Book Report Project

Literature Skill Focus: Summarizing and illustrating a story

1. Teaching the Literature Skill

- Show students a selection of numerous books, including both picture books and novels.

- Discuss with students the information that all of the book covers have in common, such as title, author, illustrator, publisher, and author and illustrator biographies. Draw students' attention to the summary of the story. This summary is written to entice potential readers to select the book.

2. Modeling the Book Project

- Demonstrate how to use butcher or shelf paper to make a book jacket. Use a book you have read to the class.

3. Reading Independently

- Have students choose a book from the library. They take the book home to read independently.

- After reading, each student makes a new jacket for the book. Students return the books and the new jackets to school.

4. Sharing the Book Projects

- When the book projects have been returned, set up a display and allow time for students to share their work.

How to Make a Book Jacket

1. Cut a rectangle of shelf or butcher paper large enough to cover the book. Leave an extra 4" (10 cm) on each of the long ends of the rectangle.

2. Fold and crease the ends of the rectangle to fit the width of the book. Fold the 4" (10 cm) flaps inside the front and back covers.

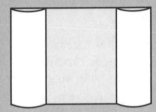

3. Try on the jacket for size.

4. Remove the jacket. Add the appropriate book information to the jacket. Include a summary of the book, as well as illustrations. Outline the title in a dark color.

A New Jacket
Individual Book Report Project

1. Use this form to record information about the book.
2. Make a new book jacket for the book.
3. When the new jacket is done, tape this form on the back of the book jacket.

Title:

Author:

Illustrator:

Statement about the story:

This project completed by

_____

File Folder Diorama

Individual Book Report Project

Literature Skill Focus: Identifying the setting and characters of a story

1. Teaching the Literature Skill

- Review with students the elements of the setting of a story. The setting is the time and place in which a story occurs.

- Read the beginning pages of *The Moon of the Bears* by Jean Craighead George. As you read, ask students to listen for clues to the setting. Some of the clues are: February, thaw and freeze, Appalachian Mountains, Tennessee, a hollow log in the wilderness.

- If your students are not familiar with dioramas, show them a sample and explain that a diorama represents a scene. A diorama shows the setting of the scene.

- Ask students to identify items that could represent the setting of the beginning of *The Moon of the Bears*, such as snowy mountains, trees, and a hollow log. Students may also suggest adding a female black bear.

2. Modeling the Book Project

- Demonstrate how to make a file folder diorama. Then add the details your class suggested for *The Moon of the Bears*.

3. Reading Independently

- Have students choose a fiction book from the library. They take the book home to read independently.

- After reading, each student makes a file folder diorama. Students return the books and the dioramas to school.

4. Sharing the Book Projects

- When the book projects have been returned, set up a display and allow time for students to share their work.

How to Make a File Folder Diorama

1. Open the file folder and refold it horizontally.

2. Cut along the original fold line as shown.

3. Color the top sections of the folder to represent the sky or the walls of a building. Color the bottom to represent the ground or floor.

4. Overlap the cut sections to form the base of the diorama, as shown. Clip them together with a large paper clip.

5. Add cutouts to represent parts of the setting and the main character.

6. Fill in the form on page 39, cut it out, and then glue it onto the back of the diorama.

How to Report on Books • EMC 6009 • © Evan-Moor Corp.

File Folder Diorama
Individual Book Report Project

1. Open the file folder and refold it horizontally.
2. Cut along the original fold line to the new fold line.
3. Color the background and the bottom of the diorama.
4. Overlap the cut sections to form the base. Clip them together with a large paper clip.
5. Add cutouts of the main character and the setting.
6. Complete this form and glue it onto the back of your diorama.

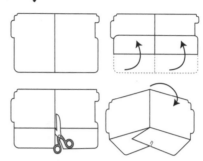

Title:

Author:

Setting:

Characters:

Write a few sentences to tell how the setting is important to the story.

This project completed by:

Main Idea Collage
Individual Book Report Project

Literature Skill Focus: Illustrating the main idea

1. Teaching the Literature Skill

- Read *A Day's Work* by Eve Bunting to your class. The book tells about a young Mexican-American boy who tries to help his grandfather find work. The boy discovers that even though his grandfather doesn't speak English, the old man has honesty and integrity.

- Help students identify this main idea. Brainstorm images or pictures that represent the main idea and the action. Students might suggest little clumps of plants, dirt, $60, a white van, a Lakers' cap, the sun, etc.

- Ask students to name a few meaningful words that are important to the story, such as *hard work, honesty, trust,* and *second chances.*

2. Modeling the Book Project

- Using some of the images students have suggested, create a collage. Cut some pictures from magazines and draw others. Arrange the pictures into a design and glue them onto the paper. Add words to the collage.

3. Reading Independently

- Have students choose a fiction book from the library. They take the book home to read independently.

- After reading, each student makes a collage representing the main idea in the book. Students return the books and the collages to school.

4. Sharing the Book Projects

- When the book projects have been returned, set up a display and allow time for students to share their work.

How to Make a Main Idea Collage

1. Fill in the planning sheet on page 41.

2. Decide on the main idea of the story. Think of pictures and words that are important to the main idea.

3. Draw pictures or cut them out of magazines.

4. Arrange the pictures into a design on a 9" x 12" (23 x 30.5 cm) sheet of construction paper.

5. Add words to the collage.

Main Idea Collage
Individual Book Report Project

1. Fill out the planning sheet.
2. Use it to help you as you create a collage about the main idea in the book you read. Draw pictures or cut them out of magazines. Glue all the pictures onto a background. Add words to the collage.
3. Cut out the form and glue it onto the back of the collage.

Title:

Author:

Illustrator:

Main Idea:

Important Pictures and Words:

This project completed by:

Comic Strip Conversations

Individual Book Report Project

Literature Skill Focus: Retelling an important message

1. Teaching the Literature Skill

- Show students an example of a newspaper comic strip. Discuss the components of a comic strip. A comic strip has three, four, or five frames, conversation in speech bubbles, limited narration at the top or bottom of a frame, and humor or satire.

- Explain that in this book report project, students will choose an important message from their book, then retell that message in a comic strip.

- Read *The Table Where Rich People Sit* by Byrd Baylor. The book tells the story of a girl who discovers that her family chooses to value their experiences with nature rather than monetary rewards. Have students suggest an important message, such as money isn't the most important thing.

2. Modeling the Book Project

- Draw a series of three, four, or five squares on a chart or the chalkboard.

- Have students suggest pictures to draw in each square to make a comic strip.

3. Reading Independently

- Have students choose a fiction book from the library. They take the book home to read independently.

- After reading, each student makes a comic strip representing an important message in the book. Students return the books and the comic strips to school.

4. Sharing the Book Projects

- When the book projects have been returned, set up a display and allow time for students to share their work.

How to Make a Comic Strip

1. Choose a message from the book. Think of three, four, or five pictures that will explain the message.

2. Cut 3" (7.5 cm) squares of paper to make the frames for the comic strip. Draw one picture in each comic strip frame.

3. Add conversation in speech bubbles.

4. Add narration at the top or bottom as needed.

5. Glue the squares onto a folded strip of newspaper.

6. Fill in the form on page 43, cut it out, and then glue it to the back of the comic strip.

Comic Strip Conversations

Individual Book Report Project

1. Make a comic strip to tell an important message in your book. Draw the pictures on 3" (7.5 cm) squares of paper. Add conversation in speech bubbles and narration at the top or bottom.

2. Fold a strip of newspaper. Glue the squares in order on the strip.

3. Fill out the information on this form. Cut it out and glue it to the back of your comic strip.

Book Report—Comic Strip Conversations

Title:

Author:

Illustrator:

This comic strip created by:

In the Headlines

Individual Book Report Project

Literature Skill Focus: Summarizing the plot

1. Teaching the Literature Skill

- Read *Anansi the Spider* by Gerald McDermott. This is an Ashanti trickster tale.

- Ask students to identify the who, what, where, and when of the story action. For example: Who—Anansi and his 6 sons; What—Anansi fell into a river and was swallowed by a fish; Where—a river in Ghana, West Africa; When—long ago. Record their responses.

2. Modeling the Book Project

- With the class, share a headline article from the newspaper. Tell students that the important information is presented in the first paragraph.

- Model how to write a newspaper article that reports the action of *Anansi the Spider*. For example:

Anansi Rescued by Sons

Yesterday the famous adventurer Anansi fell into a river and was swallowed by a fish. See Trouble, one of Anansi's sons, recognized the danger immediately and hurried with his brothers to rescue their father. The brothers used all of their talents to rescue their father. The family returned safely home to the forest. The father wanted to reward his sons for saving him. He called on Nyame, the god of all things, for help. Nyame took the great ball of light into the sky.

3. Reading Independently

- Have students choose a fiction book from the library. They take the book home to read independently.

- After reading, each student writes a newspaper article about an important event in the book. Students return the books and the articles to school.

4. Sharing the Book Projects

- When the book projects have been returned, set up a display and allow time for students to share their work.

How to Write a Newspaper Article

1. Plan your article using the planning form on page 45.

   - Think of a headline that summarizes the event you are writing about. The headline should
     —grab the reader's attention
     —use few words.

   - Write a rough draft of your article. Revise and edit as needed.

   - Think of an illustration that will draw attention to the article.

2. On a 9" x 12" (23 x 30.5 cm) sheet of white construction paper, write the headline in bold letters. Copy the article below the headline. Add an illustration to complete the article.

3. Cut out the planning form and glue it to the back of your newspaper article.

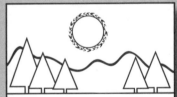

Anansi Rescued by Sons

Yesterday the famous adventurer Anansi fell into a river and was swallowed by a fish. See Trouble, one of Anansi's sons, recognized the danger immediately and hurried with his brothers to rescue their father. The brothers used all of their talents to rescue their father. The family returned safely home to the forest. The father wanted to reward his sons for saving him. He called on Nyame, the god of all things, for help. Nyame took the great ball of light into the sky.

In the Headlines
Individual Book Report Project

1. Use the form to plan your newspaper article.
2. Write the headline and the article, then draw an illustration on the sheet of construction paper.
3. Cut out the form and glue it to the back.

In the Headlines—A Book Report

Title:

Author:

Illustrator:

Headline:

Idea for Illustration:

This project completed by:

Dear...
Individual Book Report Project

Literature Skill Focus: Writing a friendly letter about a story event

1. Teaching the Literature Skill

- Ask students how they communicate news to their friends. Responses might be phone them, talk to them, e-mail them, write a note, etc.

- Read chapter I of *Ramona's World* by Beverly Cleary. In this book, nine-year-old Ramona faces the challenges of fourth grade. In the first chapter, she is proudly announcing the arrival of her new baby sister.

2. Modeling the Book Project

- Demonstrate how to make the envelope for the letter.

- On a chart or the chalkboard, write a letter from Ramona that tells about Roberta's arrival. For example,

  Dear Anne,

  You'll never guess what happened at my house over the summer. My mother had a baby! I have a new sister named Roberta. She's named after my father, Robert. She has brown hair and big brown eyes. She is so tiny. She has tiny toes and tiny eyebrows and big smiles! I wish you could meet her.

  Love,
  Ramona

- Fold the letter and place it in the envelope.

3. Reading Independently

- Have students choose a fiction book from the library. They take the book home to read independently.

- After reading, each student writes a letter from one of the characters announcing an accomplishment or describing a story event. Students return the books and the letters to school.

4. Sharing the Book Projects

- When the book projects have been returned, set up a display and allow time for students to share their work.

How to Write a Friendly Letter from a Character

1. Decide which character will write the letter. Consider that character's point of view. Pick an event that the character would want to announce or tell about.

2. Write a rough draft of your letter.

3. Follow friendly-letter format and copy the letter onto a sheet of paper.

4. Add a border.

5. Cut out, fold, and glue the envelope. Write your address on the envelope. Use the character's name and information for the return address.

6. Fold the letter and place it in the envelope.

Dear...
Individual Book Report Project

1. Write a letter from a character in your book.
2. Make the envelope. Fold the letter and put it in the envelope.

Completed by _____

Author _____

Title _____

Return Address:

_____

_____

_____

fold

fold
glue

fold
glue

A Book Mobile
Individual Book Report Project

Literature Skill Focus: Identifying story elements

1. Teaching the Literature Skill

- Briefly review with students the elements of setting and characters. Introduce the terms *problem* and *solution*. The problem presents something that is wrong or troublesome, especially for the main character. The solution is the main character's way of dealing with the problem.

- Read *Three Sacks of Truth* by Eric Kimmel. This is a retelling of a French folk tale about a poor young man who seemingly has won the hand of a princess. Her father, a dishonest king, goes back on his promise.

- Have students identify the setting, characters, problem, and solution in the book. For example,

  Setting: kingdom in France, long ago
  Characters: Petit Jean, his brothers, princess, king, queen, old woman
  Problem: king goes back on his word and demands three sacks of truth
  Solution: Petit Jean presents the king with three sacks of truth and marries the princess

2. Modeling the Book Project

- Demonstrate how to make a book report mobile using the information from *Three Sacks of Truth*.

- Hang the mobile in the classroom.

3. Reading Independently

- Have students choose a fiction book from the library. They take the book home to read independently.

- After reading, each student makes a mobile for the book. Students return the books and the mobiles to school.

4. Sharing the Book Projects

- When the book projects have been returned, set up a display and allow time for students to share their work.

How to Make a Book Mobile

1. Fill in the information on page 49. Mount the whole page on construction paper and cut out the pieces. After the glue dries, draw an illustration on the back of each shape.

2. Staple the long strip to form a ring.

3. Punch a hole in the top of each small rectangle. Tie an 8" (20 cm) string to each one. Tape the strings to the inside of the ring at even intervals.

4. Tape three more strings to the top of the ring. Bring the strings together and tie a knot.

5. Hang the mobile.

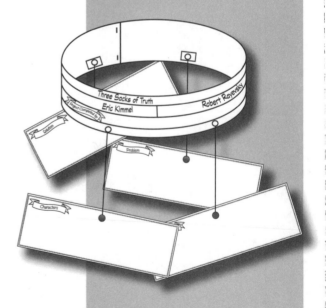

How to Report on Books • EMC 6009 • © Evan-Moor Corp.

A Book Mobile
Individual Book Report Project

1. Fill in all the information. Mount the shapes on construction paper. Cut them out.
2. Make the long strip into a ring.
3. Attach the smaller rectangles to the ring with strings.
4. Add strings for hanging the mobile.

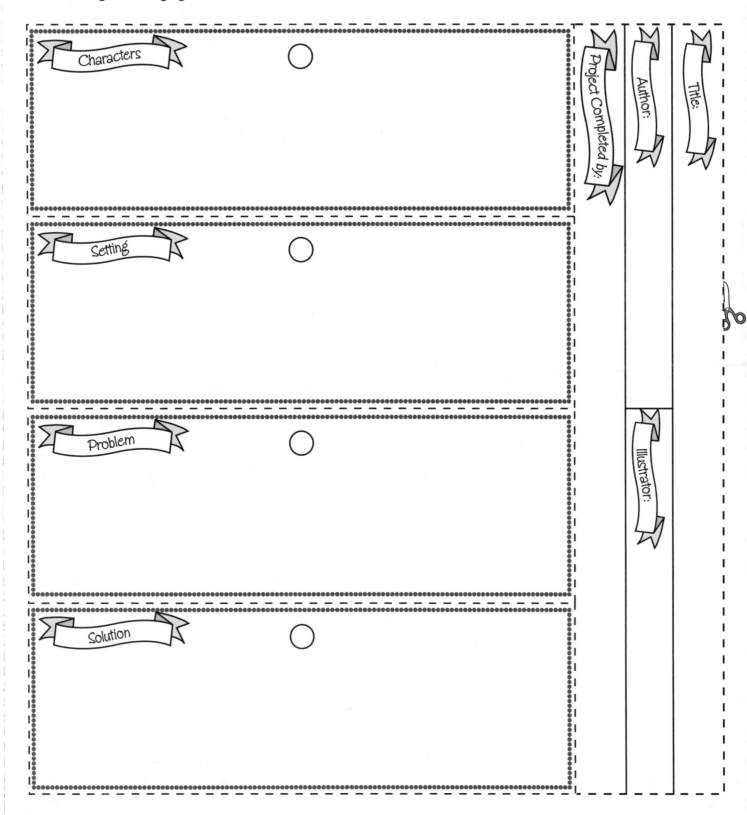

A Wanted Poster

Individual Book Report Project

Literature Skill Focus: Describing a character

1. Teaching the Literature Skill

- Remind students that readers learn about characters through the author's descriptions, the character's own words and actions, and the words and actions of other characters.

- Read *The Stranger* by Chris Van Allsburg. This is a mysterious story about a farmer and his family who take a hermit into their home.

- Brainstorm the information that students learned about the stranger. Record their responses. Students might say that the stranger doesn't know how to talk, rabbits aren't afraid of him, he works hard, he can't remember who he is, he likes being around the family, etc.

2. Modeling the Book Project

- Using the brainstormed information, demonstrate how to make a wanted poster for the stranger.

- Post the finished project where the students' posters will be displayed when they are returned.

3. Reading Independently

- Have students choose a fiction book from the library. They take the book home to read independently.

- After reading, each student makes a wanted poster. Students return the books and the posters to school.

4. Sharing the Book Projects

- When the book projects have been returned, set up a display and allow time for students to share their work.

How to Make a Wanted Poster

1. Fill in the information on the form on page 51. Color the letters in the word WANTED!

2. Crumple and flatten a brown paper bag. Cut a 9" x 12" (23 x 30.5 cm) sheet from the bag.

3. Glue the completed form to the brown paper.

4. Draw the character's picture in the center.

How to Report on Books • EMC 6009 • © Evan-Moor Corp.

A Wanted Poster
Individual Book Report Project

1. Fill in the information.
2. Cut out the form and glue it to a sheet of brown paper bag.
3. Draw the character.

WANTED!

Character's Name:

Description:

Last Seen:

Reward:

This poster created by:

A Character Puppet

Individual Book Report Project

Literature Skill Focus: Retelling a story from a character's point of view

1. Teaching the Literature Skill

- Read *Akiak* by Robert J. Blake. This is the story of a ten-year-old lead dog who has never won the Iditarod.

- Briefly review the term *point of view*. The point of view is the angle from which the story is told. A story can be told from the first person, as in an autobiography, or from the third person, using a narrator.

- Have students identify the point of view in *Akiak*. In *Akiak,* the story is told by a narrator who is observing. Discuss how the story, or an account of a story event, would be different if it were told from a different point of view. For example, how would the story have changed if it had been told from Mick's or Akiak's point of view?

2. Modeling the Book Project

- Demonstrate how to use the templates on page 53 to make a puppet of Mick from *Akiak*. Make sure that the students know that the puppet is a profile view of the character.

- Use the puppet to retell a portion of the story.

3. Reading Independently

- Have students choose a fiction book from the library. They take the book home to read independently.

- After reading, each student chooses a character, makes a puppet to represent the character, and prepares to retell the story from that character's point of view. Students return the books and the puppets to school.

4. Sharing the Book Projects

- When the puppets and books have been returned, display them and allow time for students to retell the story from their character's point of view.

How to Make a Character Puppet

1. Create your puppet on page 53. Lightly sketch details to make the pattern shapes look like the character.

2. Glue the puppet pieces to construction paper. Color and cut out the pieces. Glue or tape the book report form to the back of the puppet's body.

3. Punch holes where marked. Connect the arm pieces with paper fasteners. Attach the arm to the puppet.

4. Tape straws to the puppet: one straw to the leg area and one straw to the hand.

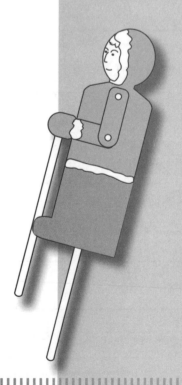

A Character Puppet
Individual Book Report Project

1. Fill in the information on the form. Draw the character using the body shape.
2. Glue the puppet pieces to construction paper. Color and cut out the pieces.
3. Glue the form to the back of the puppet. Punch holes.
   Insert paper fasteners to connect the pieces. Tape straws
   to the back of the puppet's hand and leg area.

A Book Report

Title:

Author:

Illustrator:

This project completed by:

A Cross-Legged Character

Individual Book Report Project

Literature Skill Focus: Identifying who, what, where, when, and why

1. Teaching the Literature Skill

• Read *The Last Dragon* by Susan Miho Nunes with your class. The story tells about a young Chinese-American boy who is sent to spend the summer in Chinatown with Great Aunt.

• Help your students analyze the restoration of the dragon. Have students identify the characters involved and the setting of the event. Then ask them why the characters restored the dragon and what effect the restoration had on the rest of the story.

2. Modeling the Book Project

• Demonstrate how to make a cross-legged character. Add details to make the character look like the one you are using as a model. Fill in the Who? What? Where? When? and Why? slips for the restoration of the dragon.

• Place the slips in the cross-legged character's pocket.

3. Reading Independently

• Have students choose a book from the library. They take the book home to read independently.

• After reading, each student identifies an important story event in the book, makes a cross-legged character, and identifies the important elements. Students return the books and the cross-legged characters to school.

4. Sharing the Book Projects

• When the book projects have been returned, set up a display and allow time for students to share their work.

How to Make a Cross-Legged Character

1. Begin with a 9" (23 cm) square of construction paper. Follow the steps on page 55 to make the basic cross-legged form.

2. Use scraps of construction paper to add details, such as head, hands, hat, clothes, or tail, that make the shape into a character from the book.

3. Write the title on one leg and the author on the other.

4. Fill in information on the Who? What? Where? When? and Why? slips.

5. Cut out the slips and place them in the character's pocket.

A Cross-Legged Character
Individual Book Report Project

1. Make a cross-legged character.

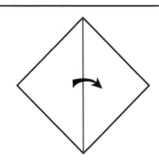

A. Fold the paper in half, corner to corner, then reopen.

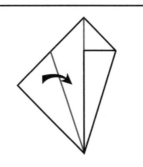

B. Fold the paper in to the center line.

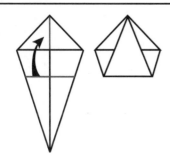

C. Fold the narrow point up to the top point.

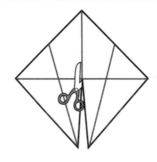

D. Open the paper and cut up the center line. Stop in the middle.

E. Refold the paper and cross the legs.

F. Pull out the pocket. Staple the legs and pocket.

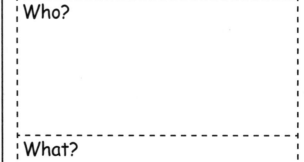

Who?

What?

Where?

When?

Why?

2. Fill in the information on the slips. Cut out the slips and place them inside the pocket of the cross-legged character.

A Character Portrait
Individual Book Report Project

Literature Skill Focus: Learning about a character from other characters

1. Teaching the Literature Skill

- Read the introductory paragraphs of *Marven of the Great North Woods* by Kathryn Lasky.

- Have students identify Marven as the main character. Ask students what the other characters said about Marven. For example, Aunt Ghisa said Marven was a boy of ten. Uncle Moishe said he was very small for his age. Papa remarked, "He's got a head for numbers."

- Discuss how these comments help the reader learn about the character.

2. Modeling the Book Project

- Demonstrate how to make a framed portrait with comments under the flaps.

- Under the flaps, write the examples of comments about Marven from the discussion.

3. Reading Independently

- Have students choose a fiction book from the library. They take the book home to read independently.

- After reading, each student draws a portrait of a character from the book. Students return the books and the portraits to school.

4. Sharing the Book Projects

- When the book projects have been returned, set up a display and allow time for students to share their work.

How to Make a Character Portrait

1. Fill in the information on the form on page 57.

2. Draw a portrait of the character inside the frame. Write the name of the character on the bottom.

3. Cut out the framed portrait. Mount it on a 9" x 12" (23 x 30.5 cm) sheet of construction paper.

4. Fold a 4" x 6" (10 x 15 cm) paper rectangle in half. Make two cuts for the flaps.

5. On the top of each flap, write the name of a character who made a comment about the character in the portrait. Under the flap, write the comment.

6. Glue the back of the flap strip below the portrait.

A Character Portrait
Individual Book Report Project

1. Fill in the book information. Draw the character in the frame.
2. Cut out the frame and glue it to a sheet of construction paper.
3. Make the flap strip. Write character names on top and comments under the strip. Glue it below the portrait.

A Character Portrait Book Report

Title:

Author: Page count:

Drawn by:

Portrait of:

A Summary Cone

Individual Book Report Project

Literature Skill Focus: Summarizing the plot

1. Teaching the Literature Skill

- Review the term *plot*. The plot is the action of the story. This action is made up of a series of events called the plotline.

- Explain to students that writing a summary is challenging. It requires selecting the most important events without retelling the complete story.

- Read *A Very Important Day* by Maggie Rugg Herold. The story tells about a citizenship ceremony that happens on a very snowy day. All the characters react to the snow differently.

- As a class, practice writing the summary. For example, On a snowy morning in New York City, families from many countries joyfully become American citizens.

2. Modeling the Book Project

- On one of the scoops, fill in the summary the class wrote of *A Very Important Day* or another book.

- Add the book information to the other scoop.

- Make the cone.

3. Reading Independently

- Have students choose a book from the library. They take the book home to read independently.

- After reading, each student makes a cone to summarize the plot. Students return the books and the cones to school.

4. Sharing the Book Projects

- When the book projects have been returned, set up a display and allow time for students to share their work.

How to Make a Summary Cone

1. Fill in the information on one of the scoops on page 59. Write a summary of your book on the other.

2. Color and cut out the scoops. Place *Here's the Scoop* on top and the summary scoop on the bottom.

3. Staple the two scoops to the top of a 9" x 6" (23 x 15 cm) piece of brown construction paper.

4. Trim the brown paper so that it forms a narrow border around the scoops and makes a cone at the bottom.

5. Draw lines on the cone. Write your name on the cone.

A Summary Cone
Individual Book Report Project

1. Fill in the information on one of the scoops. Write a summary on the other.
2. Color and cut them out.
3. Staple the scoops to a piece of brown construction paper.
4. Trim the paper to make the cone. Write your name on the cone.

staple

Here's the Scoop

_____
Title

_____
Author

staple

Here's the Scoop
A Very Important Day
Title
Maggie Rugg Herold
Author

By
Tomas

A Milk Carton Cube

Individual Book Report Project

Literature Skill Focus: Identifying the problem and solution

1. Teaching the Literature Skill

- Briefly review with students the following elements of a story: characters, setting, problem, solution, and ending.

- Read *Sarah, Plain and Tall* by Patricia MacLachlan. Have students identify each of the elements in the story. The characters are Papa, Caleb, Annie, and Sarah. The setting is a house on the prairie around 1900. The problem is that the mother died after Caleb was born. The solution is that Papa puts an ad in the paper asking for a wife. The story ends with Sarah deciding to stay with the family.

2. Modeling the Book Project

- Demonstrate how to make a milk carton cube.

- Model how to cover the cube and add panels to report information about the story.

3. Reading Independently

- Have students choose a fiction book from the library. They take the book home to read independently.

- After reading, each student makes a milk carton cube. Students return the books and the cubes to school.

4. Sharing the Book Projects

- When the book projects have been returned, set up a display and allow time for students to share their work.

How to Make a Milk Carton Cube

1. Wash two individual-sized milk cartons and dry thoroughly.

2. Cut off the tops of the two cartons.

3. Slip the two cartons into each other to make a cube. Tape the sides together.

4. Wrap the cube with a piece of colored paper, just like you would wrap a gift.

5. Fill in the information on the panels on page 61.

6. Cut out the panels and glue them to the sides of the cube.

7. With a felt pen, write "A Book Report" on the top.

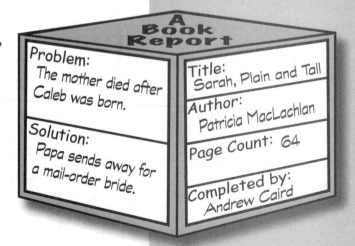

A Milk Carton Cube
Individual Book Report Project

1. Make a milk carton cube.

2. Wrap the cube in colored paper.

3. Fill in the information, cut out the panels, and glue them to the sides of the cube.

Problem:	Title:
	Author:
Solution:	Page Count:
	Completed by:
Ending:	Characters:
	Setting:

A Setting Puzzle
Individual Book Report Project

Literature Skill Focus: Identifying the elements of setting

1. Teaching the Literature Skill

- Briefly review the term *setting*. The setting includes both the time and the place in which the story occurs.

- Read *Sing to the Stars* by Mary Brigid Barrett. The story tells how one boy's love of music changes someone's life.

- Have students discuss the setting of the benefit concert. The concert took place in the city park one hot summer evening. Ask students to give specific examples that describe the time and place. They might say: it's already past 8:30; this heat; a brownout; too many air conditioners; in the darkness, the music sings to the stars. Discuss how good descriptions help the reader create a vivid picture of the time and place.

2. Modeling the Book Project

- Fill in a copy of the puzzle pieces on page 63.

- Mount the puzzle on a recycled file folder or a piece of art foam. Cut out the puzzle pieces and place them in an envelope.

3. Reading Independently

- Have students choose a fiction book from the library. They take the book home to read independently.

- After reading, each student makes a puzzle about the book's setting. Students return the books and the puzzles to school.

4. Sharing the Book Projects

- When the book projects have been returned, set up a display and allow time for students to share their work.

How to Make a Setting Puzzle

1. Fill in information about the setting and draw a picture on the puzzle pieces on page 63.

2. Mount the puzzle on a recycled file folder or other sturdy paper.

3. Cut out the puzzle pieces.

4. Place the pieces in an envelope. Write the title and your name on the envelope.

Setting
Time: A hot summer night
Description:
already past 8:30
heat
brownout
power failure
darkness
stars

Draw a picture.
Created by: David Barrera

Setting
Place: City Park
Description:
cement
park
hubbub bustle of cars and people
too many air conditioners

Title: Sing to the Stars
Author: Mary Brigid Barrett
Page Count: 28

A Setting Puzzle
Individual Book Report Project

1. Fill in each piece.
2. Glue the puzzle to a file folder. Cut out the puzzle pieces.
3. Put the pieces in an envelope. Write the book title and your name on the envelope.

Setting

Time:

Description:

Setting

Place:

Description:

Title:

Author:

Page Count:

Draw a picture.

Created by:

A Gift Package

Individual Book Report Project

Literature Skill Focus: Analyzing a character's likes and dislikes

1. Teaching the Literature Skill

- Read the first chapter of *Everything on a Waffle* by Polly Horvath to the class. Set in Canada, the story is an upbeat account of a little girl who has become an orphan. She is being cared for by a community, as well as her Uncle Jack.

- Ask students to think about one character; for example, Primrose. List students' comments about the character on the chalkboard or a chart.

- Extend the character study by asking students to think of a gift to give the character. Record students' suggestions. Ask students to explain why they picked their gifts. For example, a student might say "I would give Primrose a journal to record her recipes in because she loves to remember favorite dishes prepared by her mother and her friends."

2. Modeling the Book Project

- Demonstrate how to make the gift package using students' ideas from the lesson.

3. Reading Independently

- Have students choose a fiction book from the library. They take the book home to read independently.

- After reading, each student makes pull-down gift pages for a character in his or her book. Students return the books and the pages to school.

4. Sharing the Book Projects

- When the book projects have been returned, set up a display and allow time for students to share their work.

How to Make a Gift Package

1. Fill in the information on the gift box and tags on page 65. Write the name of the gift you would choose for the character. Write the reason the character would like the gift.

2. Color and cut out the pull-down gift package and the tag.

3. Fold as shown.

4. Punch holes in the tag and the pull-down package. Attach the tag with yarn.

A Gift Package
Individual Book Report Project

1. Fill in the information.
2. Cut out the box. Fold to make the pull-down gift package.
3. Attach the gift tag with yarn.

BOOK REPORT

The Gift:

── fold 1 ──

Why the character would like this gift:

── fold 2 ──

Title:

Author:

Page count:

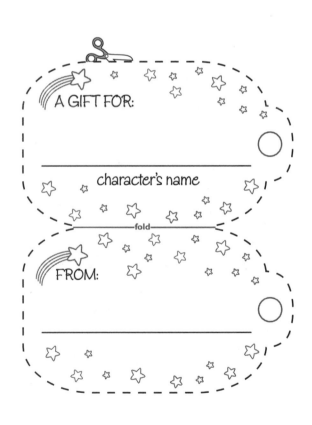

A GIFT FOR:

_____
character's name

── fold ──

FROM:

_____

The Author's Toolbox

Individual Book Report Project

Literature Skill Focus: Recognizing literary tools used by authors

1. Teaching the Literature Skill

- Explain to your class that an author uses tools just as a carpenter does. Introduce or review author's tools such as *local color, similes,* and *metaphors.* Local color is the use of details that are common to a specific place. A simile is a comparison of two things using *like* or *as.* A metaphor is a comparison of two things without using *like* or *as.*

- Read *Cendrillon* by Robert D. San Souci. This is a Cinderella story set in Martinique, an island in the Caribbean Sea.

- Have students identify examples of the three tools Mr. San Souci used. Record specific examples. For local color, students might say that he uses words and phrases from Martinique. An example of a simile is "...the girl's big foot, with toes like sausages...." A metaphor from the story is "Her smile was sunshine even when clouds hid the sun."

2. Modeling the Book Project

- Make an author's toolbox. Write an example on each carpenter's tool. Place the tools inside the box.

3. Reading Independently

- Have students choose a fiction book from the library. They take the book home to read independently.

- After reading, the student makes a toolbox and fills it with tool slips representing the literary tools the author used. Students return the books and the toolboxes to school.

4. Sharing the Book Projects

- When the book projects have been returned, set up a display and allow time for students to share their work.

How to Make an Author's Toolbox

1. Fold a 9" x 12" (23 x 30.5 cm) sheet of paper as shown. Staple the sides of the paper toolbox.

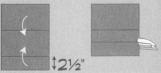

2. Fill in the book information on the toolbox label on page 67. Cut it out and glue it to the pocket of the box. Glue the larger label on the outside cover.

3. On each tool slip, write an example from the book.

4. Cut out the slips and place them inside the toolbox.

How to Report on Books • EMC 6009 • © Evan-Moor Corp.

The Author's Toolbox
Individual Book Report Project

1. Fold a sheet of construction paper to make a toolbox. Staple the sides.
2. Fill in the book information on the toolbox label. Glue it to the pocket of the toolbox. Glue the larger label on the outside cover.
3. Write examples from your book on the slips. Cut them out and place them inside the toolbox.

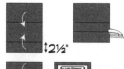
↕2½"

Name:

Author's Toolbox

Title:

Author:

Page count:

Local Color
Use of details common to a specific place

Metaphor
Comparison of two things without using *like* or *as*

Simile
Comparison of two things using *like* or *as*

A Change Pocket

Individual Book Report Project

Literature Skill Focus: Recognizing changes in characters

1. Teaching the Literature Skill

- Read *The Dot* by Peter Reynolds. *The Dot* is about a young girl named Vashti and an understanding art teacher.

- Ask your class to describe Vashti at the beginning of the story. Then ask them to describe Vashti at the end of the story. Discuss the changes that students observed.

2. Modeling the Book Report

- Demonstrate how to make a change pocket using examples from the story.

- Some books will have several characters who changed over the course of the story; others may have only one. Students may choose to add several change forms to the pocket.

3. Reading Independently

- Have students choose a fiction book from the library. They take the book home to read independently.

- After reading, each student makes a change pocket to document the changes characters underwent. Students return the books and the change pockets to school.

4. Sharing the Book Projects

- When the book projects have been returned, set up a display and allow time for students to share their work.

How to Make a Change Pocket

1. Fold a 6" x 9" (15 x 23 cm) piece of construction paper to make a pocket. Tape or staple the sides of the pocket.

2. Fill in the book information on the label. Cut it out and glue it to the pocket.

3. On the cards, write a sentence about the character at the beginning of the story and a sentence about the character at the end of the story.

4. Draw illustrations to show the character at the beginning and at the end of the story.

5. Place the cards in the pocket.

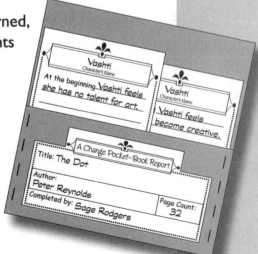

A Change Pocket
Individual Book Report Project

1. Make a construction paper pocket. Fill in the label. Cut it out and glue it to the pocket.

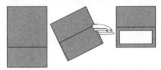

2. Make cards for the main character. Write the character's name, a sentence about the character at the beginning, and a sentence about the character at the end. Draw illustrations on the cards.

3. Place the cards in the pocket.

A Change Pocket—Book Report

Title:

Author:

Page Count:

Completed by:

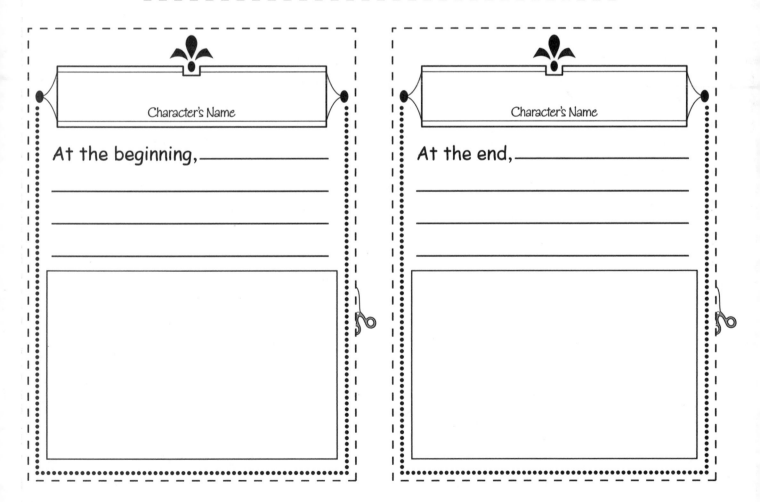

Character's Name

At the beginning,_____

_____

_____

_____

Character's Name

At the end,_____

_____

_____

Reading Strategies Bookmarks

Good Readers...	Good Readers...
•Predict Look at the title, subtitle, pictures; ask yourself what is going to happen in the story.	**•Predict** Look at the title, subtitle, pictures; ask yourself what is going to happen in the story.
•Visualize Make pictures of the words in your mind.	**•Visualize** Make pictures of the words in your mind.
•Pause/Summarize Recall the details of what you have read.	**•Pause/Summarize** Recall the details of what you have read.
•Adjust Reading Rate Read slower or faster depending on the difficulty of the words.	**•Adjust Reading Rate** Read slower or faster depending on the difficulty of the words.
•Reread Go back and read over parts that don't make sense.	**•Reread** Go back and read over parts that don't make sense.

Group
Book Report
Projects

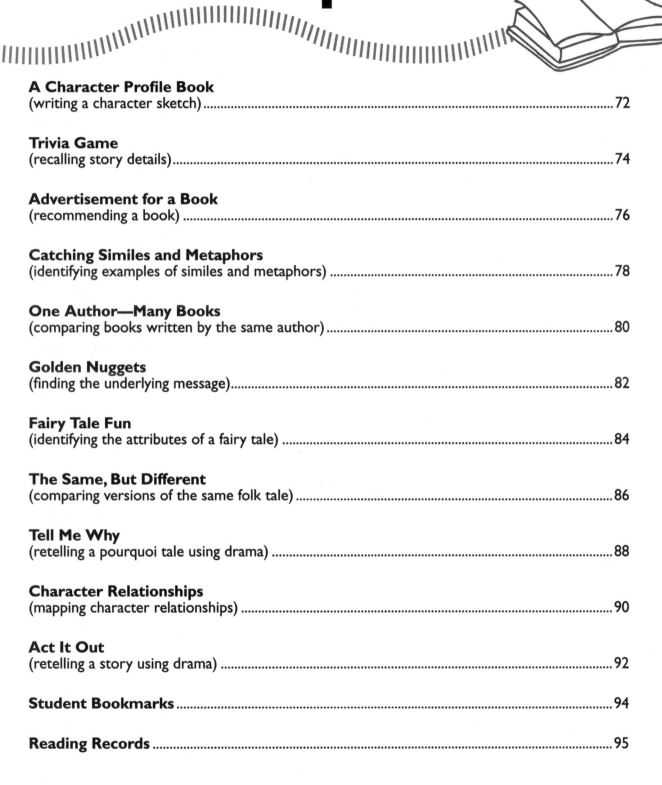

A Character Profile Book
Group Book Report Project
Literature Skill Focus: Writing a character sketch

1. Giving the Assignment
- Read brief character descriptions such as those in chapter I of *Hoot* by Carl Hiaasen. Several characters are introduced in the first chapter.

- As a class, choose a character from the chapter and begin a character profile. The characters described are Dana Matherson, the middle-school bully; Roy, the new kid in town; and the mysterious barefoot boy.

- Model how to write a brief description of a character. Ask students to recall clues to the character's preferences. For example: Roy is used to being the new kid. His dad is transferred often. He has just arrived in Florida from Montana, where he loved the mountains and snowboarding. He thinks malls are boring.

- Ask students to suggest a Saturday activity for Roy in Florida, and to support their ideas. For example: Roy would enjoy an airboat ride in the swamp because he loves the outdoors and exploring.

2. Reading with a Small Group
- Assign students to work in small groups. Select several fiction books with good character descriptions. Assign a book to each group. Provide a copy for each member. Each student reads the book independently.

- In their groups, students create a character profile. They write a description of the character and brainstorm the character's choices for Saturday activities, clothing, food, and future occupation.

3. Sharing the Group Projects
- Invite each group to present its book to the class. Display the character profile books with a copy of each book.

How to Make a Character Profile Book

1. Fill in the label on page 73. Cut out the label and tabs.

2. Stack six blank 4" x 6" (10 x 15 cm) index cards the tall way. Glue the label to the first card.

3. Glue one tab to the right edge of each of the five remaining cards. Glue them so that when the cards are stacked, all the tabs are visible.

4. On the cards, draw and write about the character's preferences.

5. Stack the cards in order. Punch holes and bind the pages.

How to Report on Books • EMC 6009 • © Evan-Moor Corp.

Trivia Game
Group Book Report Project
Master List

I think the answer is on page 77.

1. Write trivia questions and answers for your book on this master list.
2. Copy the questions onto index cards. On each card front, write the book title and page number where the answer can be found. Write the answer on the back.

Title:

Author: Illustrator:

Question	Answer	Page

Group Members:

Advertisement for a Book

Group Book Report Project

Literature Skill Focus: Recommending a book

1. Giving the Assignment

- Ask students what an advertisement is. Show several full-page ads from a magazine or newspaper. As a class, brainstorm the attributes of a good advertisement.

- Explain to students that they will be creating an advertisement for a book.

2. Reading with a Small Group

- Assign students to work in small groups. Assign books, or let students choose the books they will read. Provide enough copies of the books for each member of each group. Each student reads the book independently.

- In their groups, students brainstorm the best "selling" points of the book. They fill out the advertisement planning guide. Students create their advertisement.

3. Sharing the Group Projects

- Invite each group to share its advertisement with the class.

- Post the ads on a bulletin board, bind them into an advertising supplement, or display the books with their ads.

How to Make a Book Advertisement

1. On the planning guide on page 77, write a summary of the book. Think about the book's "selling" points. Discuss the features that would appeal to other readers.

2. Think about colors and pictures that would catch the attention of potential readers. Plan the advertisement on the planning guide.

3. Create the advertisement on a 9" x 12" (23 x 30.5 cm) sheet of construction paper.

4. Glue the planning guide to the back of the advertisement.

It's finally here, and it is definitely worth the hype! *Harry Potter and the Half-Blood Prince* by J. K. Rowling will blow you away.
No one is safe.
Nothing is simple.
Read it if you dare!

Advertisement for a Book
Group Book Report Project

1. Fill out the planning guide.
2. Make an advertisement.
3. Glue the planning guide to the back of the advertisement.

A real page-turner!

★ Planning Guide ★

Title:

Author:

Page Count:

A Brief Summary of the Book:

A Statement of Why Someone Would Want to Read the Book:

Main Selling Points:

Sketch It Here:

Group Members:

Catching Similes and Metaphors

Group Book Report Project

Literature Skill Focus: Identifying examples of similes and metaphors

1. Giving the Assignment

- Briefly introduce or review similes and metaphors.

    A simile is a figure of speech that makes a comparison using the words *like* or *as*. For example: He stood frozen like a deer caught in the headlights of the oncoming traffic.

    A metaphor also makes comparisons, but without using the words *like* or *as*. For example: She was a gazelle, clearing the hurdles with ease.

- Explain to students that in their small groups, they will be identifying examples of similes and metaphors in the books they read.

2. Reading with a Small Group

- Assign students to work in small groups. Provide multiple copies of several fiction books that have excellent figurative language. Some of these books are *Owl Moon* by Jane Yolen; *Sootface* by Robert D. San Souci; *Song and Dance Man* by Karen Ackerman; *I Can Hear the Sun* by Patricia Polacco; *Snow Toward Evening* by Josette Frank; and *The Whipping Boy* by Sid Fleischman.

- Each student reads the book independently before the group discussion.

- In small groups, students identify at least two examples of similes and two examples of metaphors. They copy the examples onto butterfly forms and attach the forms to the square as shown.

3. Sharing the Group Projects

- Display the butterflies. Take time to appreciate the examples of similes and metaphors identified by each group.

How to Make the Butterflies

1. Write the title and author of the book on the form on page 79. Glue the form to a 4" (10 cm) square of construction paper. Write the names of group members around the edges of the square.

2. Find examples of similes and metaphors in the book. Copy the examples onto the butterfly patterns.

3. Color and cut out the butterflies.

4. Tape a pipe cleaner to the back of the butterfly. Tape the other end of the pipe cleaner to the square.

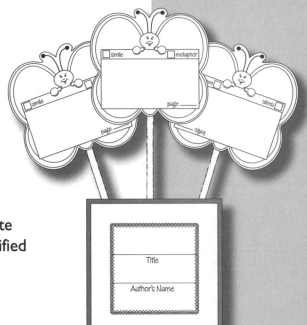

How to Report on Books • EMC 6009 • © Evan-Moor Corp.

Catching Similes and Metaphors
Group Book Report Project

1. Record the title and author on the form.
2. Glue the form to a 4" (10 cm) square of construction paper. Write group members' names around the edges.
3. Write examples of similes and metaphors on the butterflies. Color them and cut them out.
4. Attach the butterflies to the form with pipe cleaners.

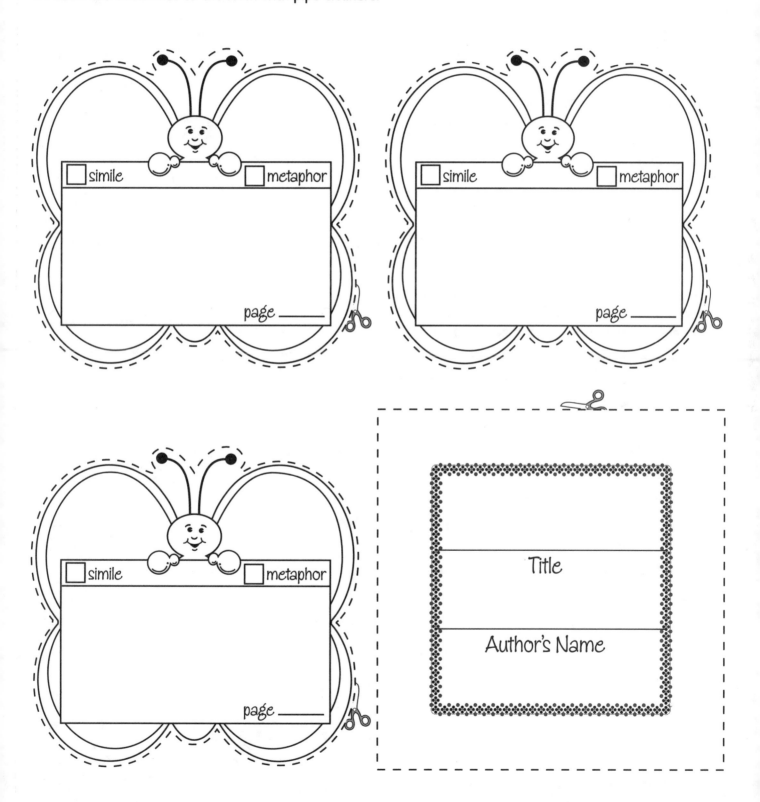

simile   metaphor

page _____

simile   metaphor

page _____

simile   metaphor

page _____

Title

Author's Name

One Author—Many Books

Group Book Report Project

Literature Skill Focus: Comparing books written by the same author

1. Giving the Assignment

- Ask students if they have ever read more than one book by the same author. Record some of their favorite authors. Explain to students that they will be writing reports about different authors.

- Review the information that students will collect, such as title, author, date published, illustrator, type of book, and a summary of the book. Using a book, show students where each piece of information is found.

2. Reading with a Small Group

- Assign students to work in small groups. Provide copies of different books by selected authors.

- Each student within a group chooses a book written by the same author, reads the book independently, and then completes the book information note taker on page 81.

- In their groups, students share the different books they have read and write an information page (biography) about the author. All pages will be bound together to create an author reference booklet.

3. Sharing the Group Projects

- Invite each group to share its author reference booklet with the class.

- Keep the booklets in the classroom library.

How to Make an Author Booklet

1. For each student, reproduce the note taker on page 81.

2. Record the information about each book on the form.

3. Each group writes a short biography of the author on a 7½" (19 cm) square of paper. Use the information on the book covers and reference books from the library.

4. Cut two 7½" (19 cm) squares of construction paper for covers.

5. Bind the biography and the forms to make a booklet about the author.

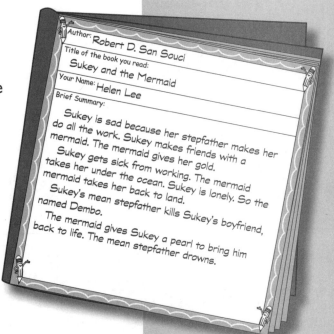

Author: Robert D. San Souci
Title of the book you read:
Sukey and the Mermaid
Your Name: Helen Lee
Brief Summary:

Sukey is sad because her stepfather makes her do all the work. Sukey makes friends with a mermaid. The mermaid gives her gold. Sukey gets sick from working. The mermaid takes her under the ocean. Sukey is lonely. So the mermaid takes her back to land.
Sukey's mean stepfather kills Sukey's boyfriend, named Dembo.
The mermaid gives Sukey a pearl to bring him back to life. The mean stepfather drowns.

One Author—Many Books
Group Book Report Project

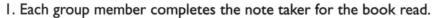

1. Each group member completes the note taker for the book read.
2. The group writes a short biography about the author.
3. Make a cover and bind the pages together to make a group booklet about the author.

Author:

Title of the book you read:

Your Name:

Brief Summary:

Golden Nuggets
Group Book Report Project

Literature Skill Focus: Finding the underlying message

1. Giving the Assignment

• Briefly review the meaning of the term *author's message*. An author's message is the underlying idea that the author is communicating. The message may explain why the characters acted the way they did, or it may be a lesson that the characters learned. A book may have more than one message.

• Read *Just Juice* by Karen Hesse. It's a story about a poor family struggling to survive. The father lost his job at the mine, the truant officer is after Juice, and the bank is about to foreclose on their house. In the middle of the trouble, the love between family members, as well as Juice's optimism, saves the day. Brainstorm the author's messages. For example: A person's worth is not determined only by success in school; you can be smart and still have trouble in school; no matter how hard it is to learn how to read, it's worth the effort; or, loyalty to family is important.

• Explain to students that in their small groups, they will be identifying the authors' messages and recording them on golden nuggets.

2. Reading with a Small Group

• Assign students to work in small groups. Provide multiple copies of books that students will read. Each student reads the book independently.

• In their groups, students identify the author's message. They write the message(s) in a sentence on the nugget forms on page 83. They mount the nuggets on a miner's pan.

3. Sharing the Group Projects

• Invite groups to share the nuggets of wisdom they found in their books. When all groups have reported, discuss similarities between the messages.

How to Make Golden Nuggets

1. Write the author's message(s) in a sentence on the nugget forms on page 83.

2. Outline the nuggets with a narrow line of glue. Sprinkle gold glitter over the glue.

3. Cut a circle of gray construction paper to make a miner's pan.

4. Write the title of the book and the author's name on the label. Cut out and glue the label to the pan as shown.

5. Cut out the nuggets and glue them on the miner's pan.

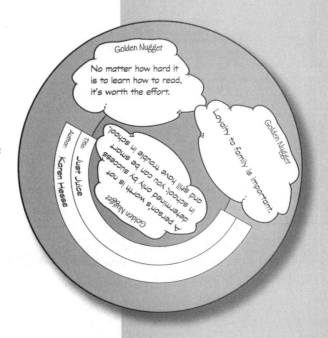

Golden Nuggets
Group Book Report Project

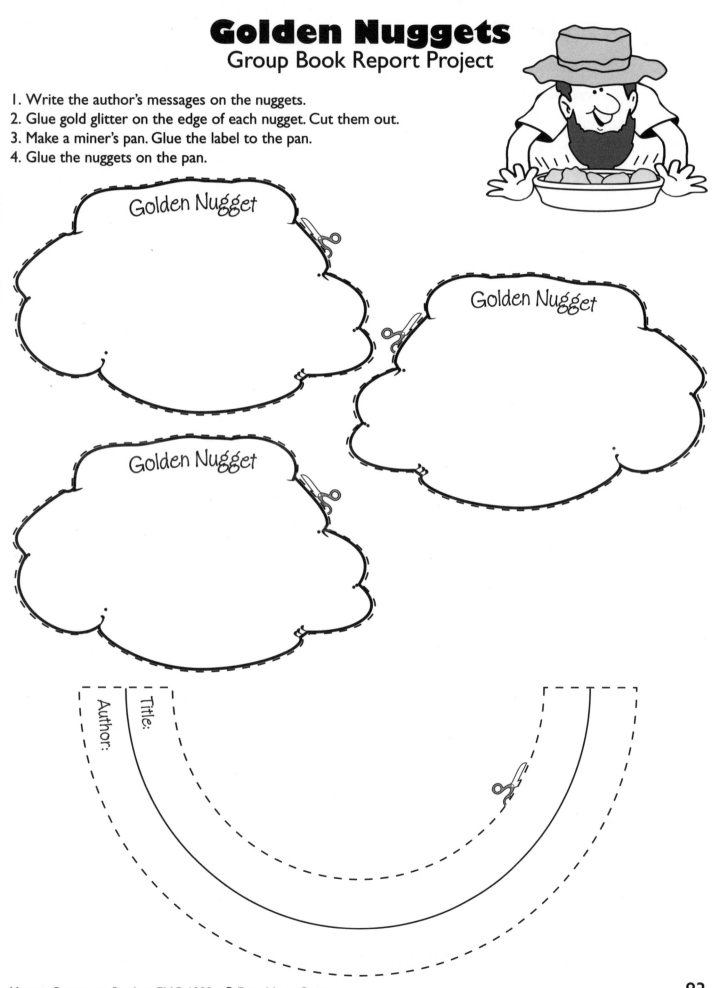

1. Write the author's messages on the nuggets.
2. Glue gold glitter on the edge of each nugget. Cut them out.
3. Make a miner's pan. Glue the label to the pan.
4. Glue the nuggets on the pan.

Golden Nugget

Golden Nugget

Golden Nugget

Author:

Title:

Fairy Tale Fun
Group Book Report Project

Literature Skill Focus: Identifying the attributes of a fairy tale

1. Giving the Assignment

- Ask students to brainstorm the attributes of a fairy tale. A fairy tale is a folk tale that involves characters that are good or evil. Good always wins over evil. Characters can be witches and queens, giants and elves, princesses, dragons, brave heroes, and talking animals. Marvelous and magical things happen to characters in fairy tales. The story usually begins with "Once upon a time...."

- Explain to students that in their small groups, they will be reading fairy tales. Each group will compare the fairy tale with an attribute checklist and make a pennant for that fairy tale.

2. Reading with a Small Group

- Assign students to work in small groups. Provide multiple copies of several fairy tales. Assign a fairy tale to each group. Each student reads the fairy tale independently.

- As a group, students brainstorm the fairy tale attributes in their book. They complete the checklist with specific examples. The group designs a pennant that represents the fairy tale.

3. Sharing the Group Projects

- Display the completed projects on a castle bulletin board with the pennants flying from the turrets.

- Point out that every fairy tale might not have the same attributes.

How to Make the Checklist and Pennant

1. Complete the attribute checklist on page 85 with specific examples from your book.

2. Make a pennant shape by cutting a 12" x 18" (30.5 x 46 cm) construction paper rectangle in half diagonally.

3. Think of a symbol that could represent the fairy tale. Draw the symbol on the pennant. Write the name of the fairy tale.

4. Tape a wooden dowel to the pennant.

5. On a turret-shaped border, display the finished checklists and pennants.

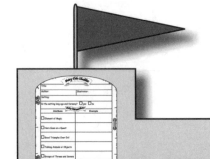

Fairy Tale Fun
Group Book Report Project

1. Complete the checklist for your fairy tale. Give specific examples for each attribute.
2. Make a pennant. Draw a symbol and write the name of the fairy tale on the pennant.

Fairy Tale Checklist

Title:

Author: Illustrator:

Setting:

Is the setting long ago and far away? ☐ yes ☐ no

Fairy Tale Attributes

Attribute	Example
☐ Element of Magic	
☐ Hero Goes on a Quest	
☐ Good Triumphs over Evil	
☐ Talking Animals or Objects	
☐ Groups of Threes and Sevens	
☐ A Character Is Transformed	

The Same, But Different

Group Book Report Project

Literature Skill Focus: Comparing versions of the same folk tale

1. Giving the Assignment

- Ask students to brainstorm the attributes of a folk tale. For example, folk tales reflect a culture. They are stories that were originally told aloud. They have been told over and over again, from generation to generation. Each time they are told, they change a little.

- Explain to students that in their small groups, they will be reading and comparing two versions of a folk tale. Then they will make a poster that reflects their ideas.

2. Reading with a Small Group

- Assign students to work in small groups. Provide multiple copies of two versions of several folk tales. Each student independently reads a version of a folk tale.

- In their groups, students fill in the comparison chart on page 87. When the chart is complete, they mount it on a poster and illustrate each example.

3. Sharing the Group Projects

- Invite each group to share its poster with the class.

How to Make a Comparison Poster

1. Complete the chart on page 87.

2. Mount the chart in the center of a 12" x 18" (30.5 x 46 cm) sheet of construction paper.

3. On 3" (7.5 cm) paper circles, draw illustrations that represent each of the sections of the chart. Glue them around the chart.

4. Record the name of each group member at the bottom of the poster.

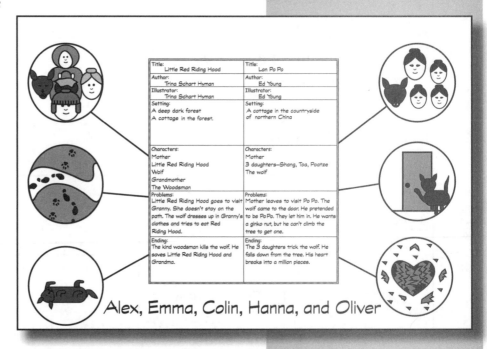

Title: Little Red Riding Hood	Title: Lon Po Po
Author: Trina Schart Hyman	Author: Ed Young
Illustrator: Trina Schart Hyman	Illustrator: Ed Young
Setting: A deep dark forest A cottage in the forest.	Setting: A cottage in the countryside of northern China
Characters: Mother Little Red Riding Hood Wolf Grandmother The Woodsman	Characters: Mother 3 daughters—Shang, Tao, Paotze The wolf
Problems: Little Red Riding Hood goes to visit Granny. She doesn't stay on the path. The wolf dresses up in Granny's clothes and tries to eat Red Riding Hood.	Problems: Mother leaves to visit Po Po. The wolf came to the door. He pretended to be Po Po. They let him in. He wants a ginko nut, but he can't climb the tree to get one.
Ending: The kind woodsman kills the wolf. He saves Little Red Riding Hood and Grandma.	Ending: The 3 daughters trick the wolf. He falls down from the tree. His heart breaks into a million pieces.

Alex, Emma, Colin, Hanna, and Oliver

The Same, But Different
Group Book Report Project

Comparing Two Versions of the Same Folk Tale

Title:	Title:
Author:	Author:
Illustrator:	Illustrator:
Setting:	Setting:
Characters:	Characters:
Problems:	Problems:
Ending:	Ending:

Tell Me Why
Group Book Report Project

Literature Skill Focus: Retelling a pourquoi tale using drama

1. Giving the Assignment

- Introduce or review the term *pourquoi tale.* Explain that pourquoi *(por-kwa)* means "why" in French. Pourquoi tales are legends that explain the why of certain customs, physical events, or animal behavior.

- Explain to students that they will be reading pourquoi tales in their small groups and acting out the tales for the rest of the class. Students will be using a model for creative drama where the narrator retells the tale. The characters act out the story, speaking key phrases when prompted by the narrator.

2. Reading with a Small Group

- Assign students to work in small groups. Provide multiple copies of each tale. Assign a tale to each group. Each student reads the book independently.

- In their groups, students discuss their tale and plan a dramatized retelling. One student becomes a narrator and retells the story. Other students act out the character parts. They perform events that the narrator describes, speaking when prompted by the narrator.

3. Sharing the Group Projects

- Invite each group to perform its pourquoi tale.

- After all have performed, discuss what you have discovered about pourquoi tales.

How to Do a Pourquoi Tale Dramatization

1. Complete the planning sheet on page 89.

2. Choose a narrator and characters from your group.

3. Practice telling the tale with characters acting out the narrator's words. Characters may speak when prompted by the narrator. For example:

   Narrator: Coyote said to Eagle,
   Coyote: I want to open the box with the sun and the moon.
   Narrator: Eagle said,
   Eagle: No.
   Narrator: Coyote grumbled, but agreed that he would wait…

   Scripts should be informal, with the narrator using the planning sheet as a guide for retelling and characters listening for narrator prompts.

4. Use name tags to identify the characters.

Tell Me Why
Group Book Report Project

1. Fill out this planning sheet.
2. Practice acting out the tale.

Retelling a Pourquoi Tale

Title:

Author: Illustrator:

Question asked by the tale:

Characters:

Main Events:

Group Members:

Character Relationships

Group Book Report Project

Literature Skill Focus: Mapping character relationships

1. Giving the Assignment

- Briefly discuss the term *relationship* with students. Brainstorm examples of different relationships between people. Emphasize the idea that relationships extend beyond the family circle to include friends, mentors, neighbors, and teachers.

- Read *Tales of a Fourth Grade Nothing* by Judy Blume. Ask students to name the main character. Then describe some of the relationships between the main character, Peter Hatcher, and other characters, such as little brother, Fudgie; baby sister, Tootsie; and neighbor, Sheila Tubman.

2. Reading with a Small Group

- Assign students to work in small groups. Choose several fiction books. Assign a book to each group. Provide a copy of the book for each group member. Each student independently reads the assigned book.

- In their groups, students make a relationship map. After the character circles are placed on the map, students record the relationships between the characters.

3. Sharing the Group Projects

- Invite groups to share their relationship maps.

- Discuss how the relationships between characters impact the story.

How to Make a Relationship Map

1. Write names and draw pictures in the character circles on page 91. Fill in the book information and cut out all the pieces.

2. Mount the circles on a 9" (23 cm) square of construction paper. Place the main character in the center. Glue the book information on the square.

3. Using a ruler, draw lines between the characters. On the lines, describe the relationships between the characters.

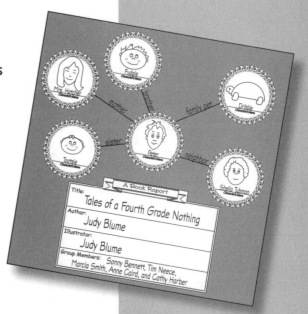

Character Relationships
Group Book Report Project

1. Complete the character circles and the book information form. Cut them out and glue them to a 9" (23 cm) construction paper square.
2. Draw lines between characters with relationships in the book. Write the relationship on the line.

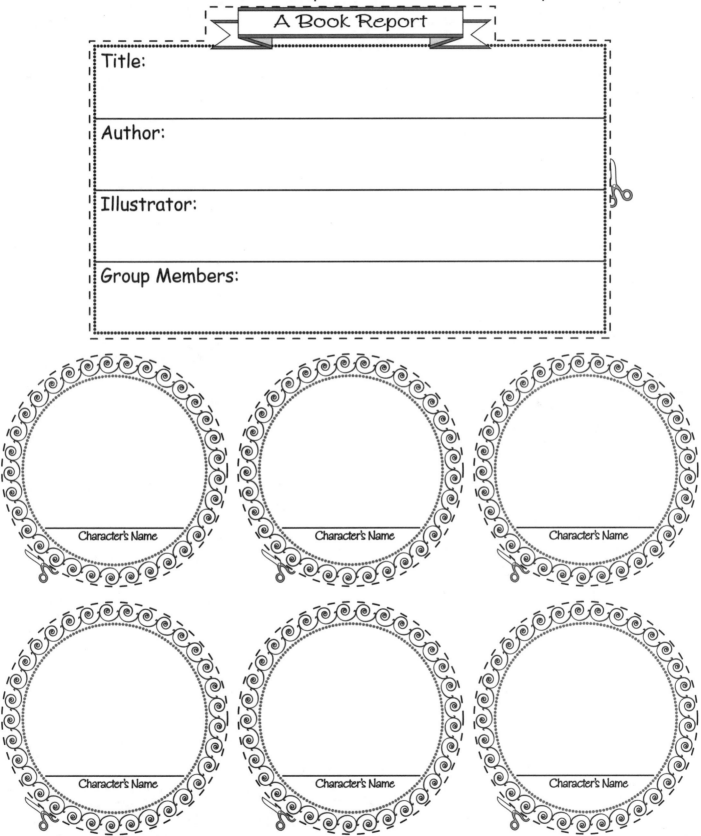

A Book Report

Title:

Author:

Illustrator:

Group Members:

Character's Name

Character's Name

Character's Name

Character's Name

Character's Name

Character's Name

Act It Out

Group Book Report Project

Literature Skill Focus: Retelling a story using drama

1. Giving the Assignment

- Introduce to students the form of drama that uses a narrator to tell the story and individuals to carry the action.

- Using a folk tale such as *Anansi the Spider* by Gerald McDermott, model how to create a storyboard to use as a script. For example, the narrator sets the scene by telling when and where the story takes place, as well as the beginning of the story. Group members will assume the roles of the characters and act out the events as the narrator tells the story. If there are any repeated words or phrases, these could be spoken by the whole group.

2. Reading with a Small Group

- Assign students to work in small groups. Assign each group a folk tale or fairy tale. Each student independently reads the assigned book.

- In their groups, students decide on the six most important events and create a storyboard. They choose a narrator and actors to act out the main events. Groups rehearse their plays and present them to the whole class.

3. Sharing the Group Projects

- Invite each group to act out its play for the class. Leave the books on display to encourage students to read new books.

How to Create a Storyboard

1. Select six key events from your story. Draw or write these events on the storyboard form on page 93.

2. Decide on one person to be the narrator. Select actors for the story events.

3. Practice acting out the story so that it comes alive.

4. Present the play to the class.

In the time of the beginning of beginnings, everything and everyone lived on Earth.

Act It Out
Group Book Report Project

Title: _____

Author: _____   Narrator: _____

Other Actors: _____

_____

Storyboard

1	2	3
4	**5**	**6**

Student Bookmarks

Guidelines for Group Book Report Projects

- Read the book assigned to your group before the group begins the project.

- Use indoor voices when you are working in the classroom.

- Respect everyone's ideas. Let everyone contribute to the project.

- One person talks at a time.

- Create a wonderful project.

Have Fun!

Guidelines for Group Book Report Projects

- Read the book assigned to your group before the group begins the project.

- Use indoor voices when you are working in the classroom.

- Respect everyone's ideas. Let everyone contribute to the project.

- One person talks at a time.

- Create a wonderful project.

Have Fun!

Name_____

Reading Record

Use this to record the books that you read.

Date	Title	Author	Comments

Reading Record

Use this to record the books that you read.

Date	Title	Author	Comments